THE FIVE EMPIRES.

The Ancient and Modern Library of Theological Literature.

THE FIVE EMPIRES

AN

OUTLINE OF ANCIENT HISTORY

BY

ROBERT ISAAC WILBERFORCE, M.A.

REPRINTED, WITH A FEW NOTES CONCERNING ASSYRIAN HISTORY

WIPF & STOCK · Eugene, Oregon

Wipf and Stock Publishers
199 W 8th Ave, Suite 3
Eugene, OR 97401

The Five Empires
An Outline of Ancient History
By Wilberforce, Robert Isaac
ISBN 13: 978-1-5326-1743-0
Publication date 1/30/2017
Previously published by Griffith Farran
Okeden & Welsh, 1899

CONTENTS.

ANTEDILUVIAN AGE.

The two races—Lamech—Enoch—Flood . . . 1

THE EARTH PEOPLED.

Nimrod—Babel 6

THE ASSYRIAN, OR FIRST GREAT EMPIRE.

Nimrod—Semiramis—Sardanapalus 13

THE CALL OF ABRAHAM. . . 16

HISTORY OF EGYPT.

Origin of its inhabitants—Sesostris—Pyramids—Necho . . 19

THE EXODUS OF ISRAEL.

Israel's typical character—The law—Preparation for Christ's Church 24

ISRAEL—ITS JUDGES, PROPHETS, AND KINGS.

Samson—Samuel—Schools of the Prophets—Solomon—Commerce of Tyre—Petra—Edom—Ports on the Red Sea—Balbec and Tadmor—Temple—Solomon's sins and punishment 27

ISRAEL AND JUDAH.

Jeroboam—New mode of worship—Ahab—Elijah—Captivity of Israel—Election passes to Judah 38

ASSYRIAN EMPIRE RESTORED.

Hezekiah—Isaiah—Prophets—Chaldees—Babylon—Its commerce and splendour—Captivity of Judah—Tyre—Apries—Prophecy of the Five Empires 44

PERSIAN, OR SECOND GREAT EMPIRE.

Cyrus—Crœsus—Oracle at Delphi—Babylon taken—Daniel—Temple restored — Cambyses — Smerdis the Magian — Darius Hystaspes—Scythian expedition . . . 59

GRECIAN, OR THIRD GREAT EMPIRE.

Office of the Third Empire—Character of the Greeks—Their independence—Their connection—Homer—Sparta—Object and measures of Lycurgus — Xerxes' expedition against Greece—Numbers of his army—Thermopylæ—Athenian character— Solon — Pisistratus—Wooden walls—Themistocles — Salamis — Platæa — Consequences of the Persian expedition 75

ATHENIAN ATTEMPT AT ESTABLISHING THE GRECIAN EMPIRE.

Spartans unfit for rule — Aristides — Athens fortified — Allies rendered dependent — Athenian and Spartan alliance — Peloponnesian war—Brasidas—Alcibiades—Sicilian expedition—Ægospotamos—Athens taken . . . 88

THE SPIRITUAL KINGDOM OF THE GRECIAN PHILOSOPHERS.

Attempt to improve man's character—Poetry and the arts—Their little effect—Plague at Athens—The Sophists—Pythagoras—Ionic school—Socrates—The four schools of his disciples—Plato—Philosophy fails of raising human nature 94

RETREAT OF THE TEN THOUSAND—THEBES AIMS AT THE EMPIRE OF GREECE.

State of Persia—Ezra—Old Testament completed—Cyrus the younger—Battle of Cunaxa—Persian treachery—Xenophon

Contents.

—Return of Greeks—Agesilaus—Thebes—Epaminondas—Improvement in the art of war—Leuctra—Laconia ravaged—Mantinæa	102

DEVELOPMENT OF THE THIRD GREAT EMPIRE—ALEXANDER THE GREAT.

Philip of Macedon—Alexander—Daniel's prophecy—Invasion of Asia—Battle of Granicus—Issus—Tyre taken—Arbela—Bactria and India invaded—Alexander's plans, and death .	107

ALEXANDER'S SUCCESSORS.

The "four notable horns"—Jews—Septuagint—Antiochus Epiphanes—Maccabees—Antiochus stopped by the Romans	112

ROMAN, OR FOURTH GREAT EMPIRE.

Early constitution—Patricians—Plebeians—Invasion of Gaul—Punic wars—Hannibal—Wars with Alexander's successors—Roman character impaired—Gracchi—Marius—Sylla—Pompey—Julius Cæsar—Augustus—Universal empire—Peace throughout the Roman world . . .	119

OUR LORD'S COMING—THE KINGDOM OF HEAVEN.

Prophecies fulfilled—Our Lord's birth—Wise men—Herod—Our Lord as Prophet, Priest, and King—His Empire, wherein like the four preceding ones—Means of admission into it—Prophecies of its durability	133

THE APOSTLES—THE CHURCH ESTABLISHED.

Faith of the Apostles—Day of Pentecost—Gospel first preached to Jews—Gentile converts—Council at Jerusalem—Two orders of ministers besides the college of Apostles—St James—St Paul at Athens and Rome—Pastoral epistles—Question whether the Jewish system would continue—Decided by destruction of Jerusalem—Jews banished Palestine—Meeting of Apostles in Judæa—Universal establishment of the order of Bishops	141

APOSTOLIC MEN—THE KINGDOM OF CHRIST EXTENDED.

Difficulties of the first successors of the Apostles—Our Lord's presence with His Church—Unity the sustaining principle of His kingdom—St Clement—St Ignatius—Reasons for unity—Maintained by community in worship and ordinances—Martyrdom of St Ignatius—The Christian city—Christian patriotism—Hegesippus—Gnostics opposed by testimony of early Church—Irenæus—Great importance of Church-system in the infancy of Christ's kingdom—The Church of England appeals to its authority—Rapid advance of the Fifth Empire—Concord within, and outward protection . 152

EARLY SCHISMATICS—MONTANUS AND NOVATIAN.

Principle of schism—Montanus—Tertullian—Novatian—State of Christians during the Decian persecution—Puritans—Pacian—Christ's kingdom re-united . . . 174

THE CHURCH'S VICTORY—CONSTANTINE—THE FIFTH KINGDOM.

Reign of Diocletian — Marcellus — Persecution — Martyrs in Palestine—Constantine—Vision of the Cross—The worldly power chosen to behold it—Christ's kingdom established . 183

THE CHURCH-SYSTEM CEMENTED—THE CREEDS.

Interval of tranquillity—Arian controversy—Constantine—Vain effort to obviate discussion—Council summoned at Nice—Arians silenced—Their political intrigues—Theodosius—Council of Constantinople — Approach of barbarians — Impending destruction of the Roman Empire—Its final homage to the Fifth Empire—Close of Ancient History . 193

EDITOR'S PREFACE.

THE Rev. Robert Isaac Wilberforce, in drawing this sketch of the history of the world, designed to set forth how all the facts of human history form part of a consistent purpose and plan, formed by the Divine Counsel, for leading men on from the fall of the first creation to its Redemption in Christ Jesus, and the establishment of the Church Catholic.

In giving it again to the public, it seemed necessary to add some few notes, concerning matters upon which recent discoveries have thrown fresh light.

In these notes I desire to record my indebtedness to a small volume of British Museum lectures by W. St. Chad Boscawen, Esq., in which many inscriptions from Assyrian remains are quoted. The original notes, of authorities and the like, remain as the author left them, indicated by numbers. The few additional notes will be distinguished by an asterisk.

EDITOR.

The Five Empires.

ANTEDILUVIAN AGE.

The Two Races—Lamech—Enoch—Flood.

B.C. 4004.

"Thou art the source and centre of all minds,
   Their only point of rest, Eternal Word."—COWPER.

THE original object of man's being is sufficiently declared by the manner of his creation: "God created man in His own image, in the image of God created He him; male and female created He them. And God blessed them, and said, Be fruitful, and multiply, and replenish the earth, and subdue it" (Gen. i. 27, 28). To set forth upon earth God's image, and to rule all creatures for their happiness, man was sent into the world.

By means of that natural perfection which he had from God's image within, and of God's outward presence, which would doubtless communicate to him gifts above nature, he might have continued in this happy state. He fell, however; he was cut off from God's outward presence; and God's image within became corrupted and debased. Yet even then he was not altogether forsaken; and the course of his history declares by what means it has pleased God to renew in some measure His lost image, and to give hopes hereafter of its perfect restoration. The end of man's existence since the fall has been to compass this object; and with a view to it, he has had to learn, first, what is the weakness and degradation of his corrupted nature; and, secondly, in what manner he may regain that purity which has been lost.

A promise on this subject was given to our first parents; and as it was a promise, the attainment of which did not rest with themselves, but was to be consequent upon the multiplication of their race, therefore it taught them that the recovery of God's image was to be bestowed upon mankind not as separate beings, but as portions of a family; not as individual subjects of the King of heaven, but as joint members of His community upon earth. Thus arose human society, out of the common expectation of the regeneration of men. Its course was long, painful, and complicated; and oftentimes none but He who sees the end from the beginning could have perceived that it advanced. For if its second stage has shewn what great benefits have been bestowed upon mankind by the restoration of God's image through Jesus Christ, yet its earlier state was but a proof that mere human efforts would not suffice for its recovery. For how could human society attain any perfection, seeing that men speedily forgot the object of its existence? From which it followed, that since one half of the human race was weaker than the other, and that in each sex there were differences both in mind and body, all respect was lost for those who, as possessors of an immortal spirit, had as much right as the strongest, wisest, or wealthiest, to their place among the community of mankind. But it was reserved for the Church to loose the fetters of slavery, to preach the Gospel to the poor, and to give "due honour to the weaker vessel" in the household of God.

That such would be the state of society was obvious, even when it took its first departure from the family of the common parents of mankind. From them sprang two races—the sons of God, and the children of men—the respective forerunners of the world and of the Church. The children of Seth built their social life upon that divine system in which they were placed, and lived in expectation of the promise of the world's recovery. Cain and his family were driven out from God's presence, and sought by their own contrivance to supply what seemed irreparably lost. Society arose in both from that family-relation in which God had placed them; mankind were bound together not by voluntary agreement, but by natural affinity; and the nation was but a wider household. But though society itself had thus a divine principle, yet the contrivances which minister to it—the arts of life, the means of security—these had a human origin, and were produced by the self-interest and necessities of man. Seth dwelt with his father Adam; and when his first child was born, we read of no consequence but the establishment of God's public worship. "Then began men to call upon the name of the Lord."[1] Cain, on the other hand, whose object was to defend himself from being "a fugitive in the earth," built the first city, and called it after the name of his first-born son:[2] and the two races continue to run parallel to one another. In the time of Lamech, the seventh from Adam, the powers of human society came to a head—his children were leaders in their several ways to the herdsmen and artificers of the world: "Adah bare Jabal: he was the father of such as dwelt in tents, and have cattle. And his brother's name was Jubal: he was the father of all such as handle the harp and organ. And Zillah, she also bare Tubal-cain, an instructer of every artificer in brass and iron."[3]

These gifts were in fact but manifestations of that sovereign wisdom from which human skill, as well as human conscience, proceeds; the confused remains of that divine image which had formerly been perfectly manifest. This image was never so far effaced as not to shew the traces

[1] Gen. iv. 26. [2] Gen. iv. 17. [3] Gen. iv. 20-22.

of what it once had been. Thus the perfection of human skill was shewn in Bezaleel to be God's inspiration.[1] And even man's society had its sanction and strength from the wisdom of God. By it "kings reign, and princes decree justice."[2] But that the worldly seed should be allowed to work out and develop these gifts of God,—that it should bring society to its strength, should build cities, and provide the arts which defend and adorn them,—is a proof that there is a certain maturity of man's social state, which is to be brought about through human agency. This Lamech beheld in the labours of his children, and to it probably he referred when he compared the security of himself, the seventh from Adam, with that of the first founder of city-life. He had heard of God's sentence on Cain; but he derided it, when he thought of the strength and ingenuity of his family, and of the safety which society conferred. "If Cain shall be avenged sevenfold, surely Lamech seventy and sevenfold."[3]

Far different was the confidence which, in the same generation, was displayed by the descendant of Seth. The dispositions of men already indicated that the advancement of civil society would be attended by a neglect of its real end. But in this very generation did God raise up a testimony to the reality of His moral government, and to the vanity of all attempts at improvement in which He was forgotten. "Enoch, the seventh from Adam, prophesied

---

[1] Ex. xxxi. 3. [2] Prov. viii. 15.

[3] Gen. iv. 24. [See upon this passage the Revised Version, and Marg. Ref. It has been suggested with great ingenuity that the true translation of this difficult text (v. 23) is, "I will slay a man for wounding me, and a young man for bruising me," and that it denotes the invention of the sword, or some other weapon, in his confidence in which Lamech boasted to his wives of his new means of protecting himself from injury. If this be correct, as seems very probable, it would indicate that in the family of Cain grew up the weapons of warfare: and that Lamech's reference is to this particular development. —ED.]

concerning these, saying, Behold, the Lord cometh with ten thousand of His saints, to execute judgment upon all, and to convince all that are ungodly among them of all their ungodly deeds which they have ungodly committed, and of all their hard speeches which ungodly sinners have spoken against Him." [1] "And Enoch walked with God: and he was not; for God took him." [2]

Thus early were the principles of human society and the hallowed rule of heavenly contemplation brought into opposition with one another. Both arise from those natural relations with which God has formed mankind, and from those powers and endowments which He has given. But they speedily took their leave of one another. Yet the happiness of man's life depends upon their moving together with an equal pace; and the complete establishment of Christ's kingdom implies their perfect combination. And the great object of history is to shew how these powers diverged from one another, and how they have again been brought to unite: their times of meeting are the grand epochs in the annals of mankind.

Before the flood these powers of the world and the Church were altogether divided. In one family God was worshipped; and Adam's life of nine hundred and thirty-one years enabled him to testify God's works to eight generations of his children. Methuselah, his descendant in the eighth generation, lived 969[*] years, so that he could talk with Noah his grandson, and with the children of Noah, and tell them what the first man had declared to

---

[1] Jude 14, 15.   [2] Gen. v. 24.

[*] Methuselah's 969 years of life bring his death into coincidence with the date of the deluge. Thus—

    Methuselah, 187, begat Lamech. Gen. v. 25.
    Lamech,   182, begat Noah. Gen. v. 28.
    Noah,   600, enters Ark. Gen. vii. 11.

    Total,   969 years: Lamech's death was five years earlier. Gen. v. 30.—ED.

him. But out of this household God was forgotten: "All flesh had corrupted his way upon the earth."[1] Even the worldly purposes of human society were destroyed. It did not yield present security. "The earth was corrupt before God, and the earth was filled with violence. And God said unto Noah, The end of all flesh is come before me; for the earth is filled with violence through them; and, behold, I will destroy them with the earth. But Noah found grace in the eyes of the Lord."[2]

———o———

THE EARTH PEOPLED.

Nimrod—Babel.

B.C. 2348.   A.M. 1656.

> "The breath of Heaven has blown away
> What toiling earth had pil'd,
> Scattering wise heart and crafty hand,
> As breezes strew on ocean's sand
> The fabrics of a child."—*Christian Year*.

THE flood is the first great epoch in history; for by it God destroyed the worldly race, and the chosen family became the representatives of mankind. God saved them "in the ark from perishing by water," while He brought in "the flood upon the world of the ungodly;"[3] just as "the ark of Christ's Church"[4] has since been appointed as the only sure means of preservation. This flood, and the means of man's deliverance from it, were long remembered among the different tribes of mankind; and an ancient historian tells us, that in his days there were "some remains of the ark to be seen among the mountains of Armenia, and that

[1] Gen. vi. 12.
[2] Gen. vi. 11, 13, 8.
[3] 2 Pet. ii. 5.
[4] Baptismal Service.

The Earth Peopled. 7

the pitch procured from it was employed as a charm."[1] For when the waters subsided, it was in this country, just in the centre of Asia, that the ark rested on the mountains of Ararat. Noah and his three sons, Shem, Ham, and Japheth, with the animals which they had kept alive in the ark, issued forth to occupy the empty world.*

For some time Noah's family lived together; and before they separated, a prediction was uttered by the aged patriarch, which has been wonderfully accomplished in the general arrangement of the world. Taking occasion from the want of reverence shewn to him by Ham, and from the filial duty of Shem and Japheth, Noah declared what would be the general fortune of their future descendants. To the children of Shem he promised that they should be the especial objects of some spiritual blessing, while Japheth's descendants should bear the leading part in the appropriation of this world's possessions. To Ham he gave no promise; and one of Ham's sons, who perhaps had taken part in his father's crime, he sentenced to be a servant to the children of his brother: "Blessed be the Lord God of Shem, and Canaan shall be his servant."[2] Finally, he foretold a combination between the worldly power of the sons of Japheth and the spiritual seed of Shem; and this consummation he predicted when those who possessed earthly might should take up their rest with the heirs of the divine blessing. "God shall enlarge Japheth, and he shall dwell in the tents of Shem, and Canaan shall be his servant."[3]

The general fulfilment of this prophecy will be seen in the subsequent history. So early did God mark out what should be the general aspect of the world. But the first appearance of things promised otherwise. Nimrod, the first who rose to worldly eminence, was Ham's descendant, and with his followers the empire of the East for a while

---

[1] Berosus, ap. Joseph, i. 4.   [2] Gen. ix. 26.   [3] Gen. ix. 27.

* The first record of Altar building, is found upon this occasion. Cor. viii. 20.

continued. Ham's other descendants, independently of Canaan, extended themselves over the continent of Africa, while the children of Shem continued in the neighbourhood of Armenia, and thence spread towards Syria and Arabia. The family of Japheth was more widely diffused; and, stretching towards the northern part of Asia, extended to India on one side, and Europe on the other. From which son of Noah the early inhabitants of America came is uncertain. Our knowledge concerning the rest is chiefly drawn from the likeness which there is in the languages now spoken by different nations. Thus we are assured, that we who live in Europe are more akin to the inhabitants of India than either of us are to the Arabians, because our languages are further removed from theirs than they are from one another.

This difference of tongues was not first produced, though it has since been increased, by the distance of different nations. But about five generations after the flood, proud men—the leaders, probably, of the chief families of Noah's sons—wished to build them a great city, that they might not be divided from one another. All the world, they thought, would thus be gathered into one empire, and men would not be scattered without connexion over the earth. This great design has since been set forth, and will one day be fulfilled in Christ's Church; but the kingdom desired by men was founded in pride, and ended in ruin. By God's law, authority belonged to Noah, that just man whom God had favoured; whereas this new city was the beginning of Nimrod's kingdom.[1] Noah would have used his authority as a parent to keep his children from idolatry; and, perhaps, for this reason God continued his life for three hundred and fifty years after the flood. But nothing good could be expected from Nimrod, that "mighty hunter," whose power was from strength, not from right, and who was the grandson of Ham, the least godly of those who had

[1] Gen. x. 9; 1 Chron. i. 10.

escaped the flood. God was pleased, therefore, to defeat this plan for making the earth one kingdom.* He confounded men's languages, so that they could not understand each other's speech. They were obliged, therefore, to separate into different nations. "Therefore is the name of" the city "called Babel," *i.e.*, confusion, "because the Lord did there confound the language of all the earth."[1]

[1] Gen. xi. 9.

* It is thought that the massive remains still existing at "Birs Nimrud" are relics of this enterprise. It consists of a solid pile of brick, rising in one part to an elevation of 197 feet. The upper portions of it bear evidences, in the vitrifaction of the bricks which originally formed it, of having been subjected to intense heat. Sir R. K. Porter has shewn that this heat operated from above, and was probably produced by lightning. The traditional account of the overthrow of Babel is, that it was the result of fire from heaven. Later Babylonian erections, especially the Temple of Belus, occupied the same site.

THE ASSYRIAN, OR FIRST GREAT EMPIRE.

THE ASSYRIAN, OR FIRST GREAT EMPIRE.

Nimrod—Semiramis—Sardanapalus.

"Here Nineveh, of length within her wall
Several days' journey, built by Ninus old,
Of that first golden monarchy the seat."—MILTON.

WE have seen how God defeated the attempt to establish by worldly means an universal empire. That plan was postponed till the confusion of tongues was remedied by as signal a miracle as had occasioned it, and till the time came for the establishment of the kingdom of God here below. Yet the final consummation was thus early provided for in the arrangements of society, and the order of man's public estate was made a framework which should minister to the purpose of the Most High. With this view the theatre of this world was filled up by four great empires, which prepared the way for Christ's kingdom. Of these, the first was the Assyrian monarchy. Before it was ended, God revealed its fortunes, and those of the three later ones, to His prophet Daniel; and by this means we know that they were the temporal precursors of Christ's kingdom, and that they will not be followed by any other worldly monarchy of like importance. But of this hereafter.

The first great empire was founded by Nimrod, and its original seat was at Babel, or Babylon. This we may suppose to have been about two thousand two hundred years before our Lord's coming, and one hundred and fifty years after the flood. From Babylon "he went out" to the conquest of Asshur, a son of Shem, "and builded Nineveh."[1] From the name of those they conquered, his followers were called Assyrians. Men's lives were still so long, that it is probable Nimrod was their leader for nearly two hundred years; and he was worshipped by them after his death under the title of Belus, or Bel. The next prince of whom we read was Ninus, whom pagan historians suppose to have lived about two thousand years before Christ. Under him Nineveh* became "that great city,"[2] of which we are told that its walls were three days' journey in circuit. It was the capital of the East, which by this time was well peopled. Its more distant countries, India, Bactria, and Egypt, had been settled at the time of the birth of Peleg, Shem's great grandson, and Peleg was lately dead, having lived 239 years.[3] Now, therefore, we hear of military expeditions. Ninus conquered Bactria, one of the first places in which the wealth of the world was concentrated, and in that early age the chief channel of communication with India. He was succeeded by his queen, Semiramis, to whom Babylon owed its earliest decorations. She was not more distinguished for her splendour than for her warlike enterprises; but she was defeated in an attempted invasion of India, chiefly by means of the elephants, which abounded in that country, and which they used in war. To match them Semiramis made figures "to imitate the shape of an elephant; every figure had a man to guide and a

[1] Gen. x. 25. [2] Diod. ii. 1. [3] Gen. x. 11.

* The question as to the size of the city of Nineveh is discussed by Canon Rawlinson, in his "Ancient Monarchies," vol. i., pages 248, etc. His conclusion is that the account given by Herodotus is gravely exaggerated; and that the description of it in the Book of Jonah as "a city of three days' journey," does not imply that the circuit of its walls would occupy that time; but that the delivery of the prophet's message through its streets and squares would occupy that period. The number of inhabitants quoted by Jonah, 120,000, however the phrase descriptive of them be understood, though a large population for that period, would not account for such an extensive city as "three days' journey in circuit" would imply.

The Assyrian, or First Great Empire.   15

camel to carry it. But these mock-elephants stood the shock of the real ones but a little while; for the Indian beasts, being exceedingly vast and stout, easily bore down all that opposed them."[1] The queen, who had crossed the river Indus on a bridge of boats, could scarcely escape herself, with about one-third of her men.

From this time the river Indus was the boundary of this great empire towards the south, while it possessed such part of the rest of Asia as was well peopled. And in this state it lasted for about twelve hundred and sixty years. Of its transactions in the interval we know little or nothing. Yet the long existence of this vast empire connects the first attempt of worldly ambition with those great events which God was afterwards about to exhibit among mankind. We see more clearly the several stages of the world's history—four vain attempts on the part of man at binding together all nations, and then the winding up of the mighty history in the kingdom of the Son of God.

After the Assyrian empire had existed in all about fourteen hundred and fifty years, it was broken into two kingdoms, which lasted about two hundred years longer. This took place at the death of Sardanapalus. His father Pul, and the people of Nineveh, had repented at Jonah's teaching;[2] but the whole people soon sunk back into sensuality and sin. Sardanapalus himself "exceeded all his predecessors in sloth and luxury, and led a most effeminate life, wallowing in pleasure and wanton dalliance."[3] Two of his subjects, Arbaces, general of the Median soldiers, and Belesis, governor of Babylon, having found means to enter

---

[1] Jonah iii. 2.

[2] B.C. 747. Great uncertainty attaches to the chronology of this part of history. The date here given is that assigned in Prideaux's "Connexion." The chronology commonly adopted in this work, up to the time of our Lord, is that of Blair; afterwards that of Burton, in his "Lectures on Ecclesiastical History," is generally followed.

[3] Diod. ii. 2.

the palace, where he had shut himself up among women and eunuchs, were so indignant at his degeneracy, that they rebelled against him. Sardanapalus at first opposed them with great vigour; but the Medes, a more warlike people than the Assyrians, finally defeated his army and besieged him in Nineveh. Its fortifications, however, were so strong, and it was so well supplied with provisions, that he might still have defied his enemies, had not a sudden inundation of the river Tigris destroyed a large portion of the city-wall. When Sardanapalus saw that his kingdom was lost, and Nineveh his great city taken, he caused a huge pile of wood to be made in his palace-court, heaped upon it his gold, silver, and royal apparel, and gathered his wives and the corrupt courtiers who had shared his excesses into the midst. Then he set fire to the pile, and burnt himself and them together. So miserable an end had a life of sin.

---o---

THE CALL OF ABRAHAM.

"Great grace that old man to him given had,
For God he often saw from heaven's height."

SPENSER.

ABOUT the time when the first worldly empire came to its strength under Semiramis, it pleased God, with whom a thousand years are as one day, to make gradual and silent preparation in another manner for that kingdom in which the nations of this world were finally to be united. This was done by the call of Abraham. Abraham was the chief of one of the eldest tribes of Shem's children; and though even among them the worship of idols had begun to

The Call of Abraham.

appear,[1] yet the God of Noah was remembered in this family,[2] which had remained at Ur in Chaldea, near man's first dwelling-place, and which probably had long been influenced by the neighbourhood of Noah himself. From this country, now become the seat of the Babylonian empire, Abraham was called to depart.[3] "The Lord had said unto him, Get thee out of thy country, and from thy kindred, and from thy father's house, unto a land that I will shew thee: and I will make of thee a great nation, and I will bless thee, and make thy name great, and thou shalt be a blessing: and I will bless them that bless thee, and curse him that curseth thee: and in thy seed shall all the nations of the earth be blessed."[4]

This promise is the great charter of the Church. When Adam lost Paradise, God had promised him, that of the woman's seed should come a deliverer for the human race.[5] And now the hope was to gain shape and substance, by being embodied in those lasting institutions which have their completion in the Church. The promise makes mention, first, of an earthly inheritance, and then of a heavenly possession; first of a temporal seed, and then of a spiritual progeny; first of that which should be confined to one nation, and then of that in which all the world should be included. Yet were these several parts of the promise so united, that the one was borne, as it were, in the arms of the other. Before their completion they seemed but one, and since their completion they have been again so blended together, that whatsoever was spoken of the outward, has reference also to the inward blessing. For God's dispensations have been ever thus; what is present and temporal has taken its shape from some more lasting blessing which lay hid within. As the indistinct imaginations of childhood express the weakness of man's knowledge in this present

---

[1] Josh. xxiv. 2.   [2] Gen. xxxi. 53.   [3] B.C. 1921.
[4] Gen. xii. 1-3.   [5] Gen. iii. 15.

state,[1] and as the ark was a token of the Church, in which men are in like manner offered a refuge from destruction,[2] so was God's dealing with the temporal seed of Abraham a type, that is, an *acted prophecy*, of what befals his spiritual descendants. Thus does the whole promise of Abraham belong to the Church of Christ. For it was limited from the first to one of the nations of which Abraham was the natural parent—namely, to that nation of Israel, of which, now that men are elected not by birth, but by baptism,[3] the Church of Christ has inherited the privileges and the name.[4] "The promise," says St. Paul, "was not made to seeds, as of many, but as of one, and to thy seed," the Church of Christ;[5] that the blessing of Abraham might come on the Gentile Church.[6]

The promise, then, that it should be "the heir of the world,"[7] and that it should redress the miseries which sin had introduced, was thus early given to the Church of God; and for her sake, and for the fulfilment of God's blessing, have the long line of her patriarchs, saints, and martyrs contended. Of these Abraham was among the greatest. He left his native land, and went out, not knowing whither he went. "By faith he sojourned in the land of promise, as in a strange country, dwelling in tabernacles with Isaac and Jacob, the heirs with him of the same promise. For he looked for a city which hath foundations, whose builder and maker is God."[8] Here he afforded a memorable instance of domestic piety, setting up an altar to his God in every place of his temporary abode. And to reward his faith he had an especial vision of his great Descendant, whose coming it was the privilege of the latter days to witness. But Abraham "desired to see that day, and he saw it, and was glad."

[1] 1 Cor. xiii. 11, 12.   [2] 1 Pet. iii. 20, 21.   [3] Rom. ix. 24.
[4] Gal. iii. 16.   [5] Gal. iii. 16.
[6] Gal. iii. 14.   *Vide* "Hammond" *in loco.*   Tholuck's "Alte Test. in Neuen."
[7] Rom. iv. 13.   [8] Heb. xi. 9-11.

HISTORY OF EGYPT.

Origin of its Inhabitants—Sesostris—Pyramids—Necho.

"I must dwell longer upon Egypt, because it contains more that is remarkable, and more objects worthy of attention, than any other country. With a peculiar climate, and a river resembling no other in the world, the Egyptians have also laws and customs quite contrary to those of any other mortals."—HERODOTUS, ii. 35.

THE Assyrian empire had little to fear from the worldly might of Abraham; although, in defence of his nephew Lot, he once defeated its prince, as though in token of the ultimate superiority of his children. It was different with the kingdom of Egypt, which for many centuries threatened to divide with it the command of the East, and was not finally conquered till the time of the Persians. Nor is this the only thing which renders the history of Egypt interesting. Painting, statuary, and architecture, the art of medicine, and of what is called statistics —the art, that is, by which the inhabitants and the wealth of *states* is calculated—had their origin in that country.[1] The fables which passed from ancient Egypt into Greece have exercised great influence on literature. Thus we still retain in our language the word *phœnix;* a name derived from the early legend, that every five hundred years the bird so called came to the temple of the Sun at Egyptian Thebes, that there a spontaneous fire consumed it, and that out of its ashes arose another bird to inherit its name and nature.[2] Further, Egypt was for many years the nursery of the Israelitish race. During the infancy of that people, God was pleased to let them grow up under the shelter of Egyptian civilisation, till they were numerous enough to be planted as a separate nation among the families of the earth.

[1] Herod. ii. 177.   [2] Id. ii. 73.

That Egypt was one of the first countries settled after the flood, we gather from its being sometimes called the land "of Ham,"[1] and from its retaining in its native dialect a name derived from Ham's son, Misraim. This early settlement, before the tribes of men were widely separated, was the reason, probably, why the Egyptians had so much in common with the Indians, who are not supposed to have been the children of Ham. Among both, for example, prevailed what were called *castes;* that is to say, a man might not pass from one rank or class to another, but children were obliged to follow the occupation of their parents. The ancient Egyptian language[2] also was, in some curious particulars, a common link between that which was spoken by the descendants of Shem and Japheth. No doubt men must have been attracted to the country by the extreme fertility which is derived from the river Nile. The annual inundation of that river in the summer months, in consequence of the rains in Nubia near its source, supplies Egypt, where it scarcely ever rains, with water. The lower and more fertile part of the country, called from its shape the Delta (the Greek name of the letter Δ), is perfectly flat, and the villages are built on embankments, which during the inundation are left as islands amid the waves. Parts which the river cannot reach require to be watered artificially: hence Egypt is said to be "watered by the foot;"[3] that is, by water raised by foot-pumps, whence the unusual alarm created by those storms with which Moses was ordered to afflict it.[4] Besides the fertility which it occasioned, the inundation of the river encouraged the growth of science in Egypt, because geometry, or a knowledge of the properties of figures, was required for dividing the land which the waters had covered.[5]

[1] Ps. lxxviii. 51.

[2] Thus, in the Semitic languages the pronoun *he* is the copula; in the Japhetic the verb substantive *is*. But in the Coptic the pronoun and verb substantive are employed indiscriminately.

[3] Deut. xi. 10.   [4] Ex. x. 24.   [5] Herod. ii. 109.

History of Egypt.

At an early period of their history, the Egyptians were enslaved by a foreign tribe, probably either the Assyrians, or some people from the same quarter, who, from their occupation, were called *Hycsos*, or shepherds.[1] This must have happened soon after the time of Abraham; for when his grandson Jacob was compelled by famine to remove from Canaan into Egypt,[2] great prejudice was felt against the occupation of his family: "Every shepherd" was "an abomination to the Egyptians."[3] The shepherd-kings, therefore, had been driven out, but were still remembered. When Jacob's family first settled in Egypt, it was in number but seventy persons; but after remaining two hundred and sixteen years in that country, it had increased into a vast multitude.[4] At that time there rose up a king of a new family, who was ignorant of the services which had been rendered to Egypt by Joseph. This new Pharaoh,—so the kings of Egypt were called, from a word which signifies the sun,[5]—was guilty of those great cruelties towards Israel which God punished by the infliction of ten plagues.[6] At first he subjected them to excessive labour in preparing bricks for his treasure cities and other public buildings; and more ancient bricks have been found to bear his mark than that of any other king of Egypt.[7] But as this did not check their increase, he put their children to death, until God was pleased by a stretched-out arm to bring them up out of the house of bondage. Though this for a time weakened the Egyptians, yet they recovered their strength; and being more skilful than their neighbours in the arts of war as well as those of peace, they continued to rule over the adjoining nations.

During the time that the Israelites were governed by judges, the celebrated king Sesostris marched as far as into Asia Minor, set up columns there in memory of his victories,

---

[1] Jos. in Apion, i. [2] B.C. 1706 [3] Gen. xlvi. 34. [4] Ibid. 27.
[5] Wilkinson's "Ancient Egyptians," chap. ii. [6] B.C. 1491.
[7] Wilkinson's "Ancient Egyptians," ii. 99.

and founded a colony at Colchis.[1] Out of pride he made the captive kings whom he had conquered draw his chariot.

This was hardly a greater mark of ostentation than was shewn by other Egyptian kings, who reared as their monuments those great pyramids, which continue to this day. The principal pyramids are three in number; the largest, which is attributed by Herodotus to Cheops, is four hundred and sixty-one feet in height (about a third higher than St. Paul's), while its base, a square of seven hundred and forty-six feet, is as large as the area of Lincoln's-Inn Fields. Herodotus tells us that one hundred thousand men were engaged for twenty years in its erection.[2] The next in size were built by the successors of Cheops—his brother Chephris, and Mycerinus his son. Small chambers are found in the very centre of these buildings, accessible by narrow passages, which were designed apparently for the burial-places of their founders.

It was the common custom of the Egyptians to preserve the bodies of their dead in figured cloths, of which vast numbers, as well as of the pictures which adorned their tombs, are still to be seen. The pictures form a sort of writing, which from their being employed to describe sacred subjects, are called hieroglyphics. In them we see many things which are mentioned in the Old Testament; God having been pleased that the country where His people sojourned should be the longest remembered. We see the custom of embalming the dead, as was done with Jacob; and we find a separate class of men employed as physicians, as is mentioned in the book of Genesis. The worship of the golden calf is seen to be an imitation of what the Israelites had witnessed in Egypt. These and similar things are perpetuated by Egyptian monuments.

Though this country, commanding the entrance of the Nile, the largest river in the world, and adjoining both the Red Sea and the Mediterranean, was well adapted for purposes of commerce, yet, owing to the exclusive disposition

[1] Herod. ii. 102.   [2] Herod. ii. 124.

of its inhabitants, it was little known by the Greeks till the reign of Psammetichus.[1] He owed his throne to the assistance of Grecian mercenaries, to whom in return he gave a settlement in Egypt. His son Necho, a warlike prince, extended the Egyptian power in Asia, and captured Jerusalem, after defeating king Josiah.[2] Herodotus calls it Cadytis, or the holy city, and describes it as nearly of the size of Sardis.[3]

Necho, however, was compelled to yield to the arms of the Assyrians, and to confine himself to his own continent.[4] Here he had been engaged in constructing a canal which was to unite the river Nile to the Red Sea; an enterprise in which one hundred and twenty thousand persons are said to have perished.[5] But he left his purpose incomplete, probably because, on his defeat by the Assyrians, he feared to facilitate their passage into Egypt. He continued, however, to direct his attention to the navigation of the Red Sea; and from the measures which he employed for discovering the south of Africa, he appears to have formed designs of extending his power in that direction. For it was by his orders that some Phœnician mariners sailed down the Red Sea, with a view of discovering whether a passage could be found by it to the Straits of Gibraltar.[6] The course which they held was one in which the winds were likely to favour them; and we are told that in three years they passed round Africa, landing every winter, and setting forth again at the approach of spring. A circumstance is added, which, to the ancients, unacquainted with the southern hemisphere, threw doubt upon their testimony, but which is in reality the strongest confirmation of the truth of their narrative. They stated, as a singular phenomenon, what must necessarily happen to the south of the line, that as they sailed round Africa the sun at midday appeared to the north, and not to the south of them.

[1] Herod. xi. 152. B.C. 660.
[2] Herod. ii. 159. B.C. 608.
[3] Jer. lxvi. 2.
[4] Herod. iii. 5. B.C. 604.
[5] Herod. ii. 158.
[6] Herod. iv. 42.

THE EXODUS OF ISRAEL.

Israel's Typical Character—The Law—Preparation for Christ's Church.

> " Ye too, who tend Christ's wildering flock,
> Well may ye linger round the rock
>   That once was Zion's hill;
> To watch the fire upon the mount,
> Still blazing like the solar fount,
>   Yet unconsuming still."—*Christian Year.*

THE Israelites had dwelt two hundred and sixteen years in Egypt, and four hundred and twenty years had passed since Abraham had received the promise of the land of Canaan, when God called them to its possession.[1] They had at first grown into a great nation under the shelter of the Egyptian government; but the oppression which that government had now begun to exercise made them receive gladly the summons to depart. Moses led them forth,—a man preserved in childhood by God's providential care, afterwards instructed by God Himself in the wilderness, and finally sent back to perform by divine power what, in the presumption of youth, he had expected to accomplish by human means.

As God delivered His people by miracle from Egypt, so, by like miracle, did He preserve them in the wilderness. Forty years they remained there; they received new laws, they formed new habits, till they were ready to come forth as a separate people into the country which they were to possess. This wonderful change of the common laws of God's providence was not ordained for their sakes alone. "These things happened unto them for ensamples; and they are written for our admonition, upon whom the ends

---

[1] B.C. 1491.

of the world are come."[1] In His dealings with Israel it pleased God to give a sign of His dispensations with the Church at large. Israel was led through the waters of the Red Sea; so has God appointed that through the waters of baptism men pass into His Church.[2] As by this ordinance men are admitted into "the number of God's faithful and elect children,"[3] so was the nation of Israel "elected" to be a "special people."[4] Thus was their general predestination a sign of the election of individuals in later days to Christian privileges. So, again, the manna with which they were fed in the wilderness was a type of that heavenly food with which, in His holy communion, our Lord refreshes His faithful servants.[5] The wilderness in which they walked so long, resembled the world we inhabit; and the heavenly state was signified by the Canaan of rest which lay beyond.[6]

These things were understood not at the moment, but were "pearls that lay concealed in the great deep of God's counsels."[7] And when the Israelites entered Canaan, the old figures passed away like visions of the night, and a new series of God's dealings began. But before this happened, that wonderful law had been given, the schoolmaster to bring men to Christ, which lasted till it was fulfilled in Him. This law had several parts and many objects. Its first part consisted of those ten commandments which Moses distinguishes from the rest, because spoken by the very mouth of God,[8] by which the teaching of man's conscience, and the commands which had been given to the patriarchs, were renewed. Another part consisted of those laws and ceremonies which were meant to keep the Israelites distinct from surrounding nations. Thus were they fitted for their great purpose, to prepare the way for the coming of Christ. The provision for this object was the third and most important part of their law, which by its sacrifices led their

---

[1] 1 Cor. x. 11. [2] 1 Cor. x. 1. [3] Baptismal Service.
[4] Deut. vii. 6. [5] John vi. 51; 1 Cor. x. 3, 16.
[6] Heb. iv. 8. [7] Davison on Sacrifice. [8] Deut. v. 22.

minds to that great and only real sacrifice for sin, to be offered once for all on the cross. The sacrifice of a lamb, at the season of the passover, was the clearest type of the sacrifice of that Lamb of God, who at the self-same season shed His blood for our deliverance. But this was a type which could not be understood till it shone in the light of its own fulfilment. Other things there were which could earlier be perceived. The law, which appointed means for atoning for every outward defilement, provided no method by which the defilement of sin could be done away. Yet conscience taught that the murderer needed forgiveness more than the man who touched the dead, and that evil thoughts defiled the soul more than outward stains the body. Thus by what it left undone, as well as by what it did, the law taught men to expect a Saviour.

At this time, also, our Lord's coming was declared by clearer prophecies. Balaam, the pagan seer, who was summoned by the king of Moab to curse Israel, spoke of the "Star" which should rise "out of Jacob."[1] This prophecy was remembered by other Eastern nations also; but to God's people, their own leader, Moses, declared, "a prophet shall the Lord your God raise up unto you of your brethren, like unto me."[2] And truly, till the Hope of all nations came in the flesh, "there arose not a prophet like unto Moses, whom the Lord knew face to face."[3] The miraculous preservation of his bodily frame was a sign of that unwonted measure of spiritual strength with which it pleased God to favour him. "Moses was one hundred and twenty years old when he died: his eye was not dim, nor his natural force abated."[4] But what still more distinguished him was his willingness to sacrifice his life for the rebellious people whom he led. "If Thou wilt," he prayed to God, "forgive their sin; and if not, blot me, I pray Thee, out of Thy book, which Thou hast written."[5] In

---

[1] Num. xxiv. 17.   [2] Deut. xviii. 15.   [3] Deut. xxxiv. 10.
[4] Deut. xxxiv. 7.   [5] Exod. xxxii. 32.

this respect, as well as in his character of priest and law-giver, he was a type of that divine Being, who truly gave up His life, not merely as a friend on behalf, but also as a sacrifice instead of men.[1] Thus early was preparation made for the establishment of a spiritual kingdom; and while the civil societies of men were opening its way by the advancement of order and intercourse, God had already fixed its roots in the bosom of a religious community. Here was already afforded a miniature of the achievements of later times,—the great deeds of the Son of God fore-acted in dumb show in the ordinances of God's worship and in the history of His people. As the games of childhood foreshadow the serious actions of after-life, so were those sublime transactions, which were afterwards to be performed on the world's highest theatre, not only foretold in the words, but also foredone in the types of prophecy.

---o---

ISRAEL: ITS JUDGES, PROPHETS, AND KINGS.

Samson—Samuel—Schools of the Prophets—Solomon—Commerce of Tyre—Petra—Edom—Ports on the Red Sea—Balbec and Tadmor — Temple — Solomon's Sins and Punishment.

> " Why sleeps the future, as a snake enroll'd
> Coil within coil at noontide?"—WORDSWORTH.

WHEN the Israelites had been forty years in the wilderness, they advanced under Joshua, the successor of Moses, against the nations of Canaan.[2] These people, the most corrupt of the children of Noah, had, in consequence, been sentenced by God to total destruction.[3]

---

[1] Matt. xx. 28. [2] B.C. 1451. [3] Gen. ix. 25.

In Abraham's time "their iniquity was not yet full,"[1] though Sodom and Gomorrah were, even in that day, visited by a supernatural ruin. But now the time of their punishment was come, and the Israelites were ordered to inflict it. As the executioners of God's sentence, Israel was required to destroy those nations from under heaven. This was, in a measure, effected during the time of Joshua. The land was divided among the twelve tribes; and during the space of three hundred and fifty years they lived in it without temporal king, without settled government, distinct from all other people; at times oppressed by their neighbours as a punishment for their neglect of God's law, and then again restored by one or another deliverer upon their repentance. Meanwhile the public worship of their nation was at Shiloh, in the land of Ephraim, where the ark and the tabernacle of the congregation had been placed by Joshua.

The last of the judges who were raised up for the deliverance of Israel was Samson,[2] a man in whom it pleased God to set forth with peculiar clearness what had been in a measure exhibited in many previous leaders—how the mere earthly gifts of strength and valour may minister to His service. By using the arm of a self-willed and self-indulgent man for effecting the ends which by an irreversible decree He had ordained of old, the Almighty seemed to assert His rule over all the ordinary endowments of humanity. Nor was this lesson confined to the Israelites. By their intercourse with other nations, the fame of Samson was spread throughout the ancient world; his achievements as the deliverer of the chosen people mingled with the feeling that some gifted champion was needed to redress the violence under which mankind in general were suffering; and under the name of Hercules,*

---

[1] Deut. ix. 4; Gen. xv. 16; Gen. xviii. 20.   [2] B.C. 1161.

* The story of Hercules is now generally thought to belong to the class of legends which were designed to set forth natural phenomena

as St. Augustin assures us,[1] the deeds of the son of Manoah were remembered. In the Tyrian Hercules[2]—for the Greeks could trace him to the East—we see the miraculous birth of Samson, his conquest over the lion, his ruin by female arts, and the circumstances of his death recorded.

During the long interval in which the judges ruled, there seems to have been no progress towards those great events which formed the design of Israel's history. Yet it was obvious that the purpose of the law had not yet been attained; and all might understand that one part at least of Abraham's promise, which extended to all nations of the earth, had not been accomplished. At the end of this time begins a new period in the history of Israel; a succession of prophets who uttered fresh predictions, and of princes who gave fresh examples, of Messiah's kingdom. This period[3] was introduced by Samuel the prophet. He came in a new character, to revive what had been lost, and to prepare for what was coming. His commission was shewn by predictions, of which the fulfilment was so manifest and immediate, that "all Israel, from Dan to Beersheba, knew that Samuel was established to be a prophet of the Lord."[4]

His ancestor, Korah,[5] had perished miserably, for presuming, without authority, to exercise that priestly office which belonged to the family of Aaron. But Samuel had authority to supersede the usual ministers. For "no man taketh this honour unto himself, but he that is called of God, as was Aaron."[6] And the ordinary ministers of God under the disguise of tales about heroes and gods, called "solar myths." Like other theories, it is very likely that this particular notion has been pressed too far, and that more has been put upon it than it will fairly carry. There seems to be no reason why traditions of fact may not, by the addition of a little ingenious fiction, have been rounded off into "myths" or "parables" for this purpose. And the story of Samson may have been the groundwork on which the mythmongers embroidered the legend of Hercules.

[1] "De Civitate Dei," xviii. 19. [2] Bochart's "Peleg," p. 610.
[3] B.C. 1176. [4] 1 Sam. iii. 20. [5] 1 Chron. vi. [6] Heb. v. 4.

give place at all times to those who, by their miracles, can shew an extraordinary commission.

But not only did Samuel exercise the ordinary offices of the priesthood,—he laid the foundation of institutions by which the future condition of Israel was greatly amended. He found the people, as the last chapters of the book of Judges teach us, in its domestic habits and its daily life little raised above the surrounding heathen. How was this to be remedied? Some permanent means of instruction was needed; something which might create a better standard of feeling and practice, and might gradually imbue the whole population with those principles which are contained in the law of God. For this purpose he established the colleges of the sons of the prophets. He began with two places— one, the hill of God near Bethel;[1] the other, Naioth in Ramah, near his own residence,[2] and there collected a band of youths, whom he trained for God's service. The object of these institutions was not merely the instruction of the young. In them, as in the cathedrals of our own land, the solemn service of God was continually maintained; music and singing were employed to impress the minds of a thoughtless generation; and thus two places at least in the land displayed in its perfection that devotional character which belonged especially to the situation of God's chosen people.

These measures were calculated to produce great effect upon the character of Israel, and doubtless led the way to that increased measure of God's worship which distinguished the days of David. Samuel's own grandson was the first of those "whom David set over the service of song in the house of the Lord, after that the ark had rest."[3] Such colleges of the prophets lasted and increased during the days of the monarchy. To this institution likewise Samuel, though unwillingly, led the way; and at the desire of the people, not contented by the Almighty's immediate govern-

[1] 1 Sam. x. 6. [2] 1 Sam. xix. 20. [3] 1 Chron. vi. 31, 33.

ment, he was instructed to appoint a king. He first anointed Saul, and then David, to the royal office. And in David, who was wonderfully brought without his own seeking to the kingdom, and still more in Solomon, his son, the course of God's providence was further discovered.[1] For not only did the greatness, strength, and splendour of Solomon realise that promise of worldly power which was made to Abraham, but it afforded a figure of that spiritual kingdom which the future seed of David was to establish. Solomon also was endowed by God with a wisdom which was far more valuable than any earthly greatness. "He was wiser than all men; than Ethan the Ezrahite, and Heman, and Chalcol, and Darda, the sons of Mahol: and his fame was in all nations round about."[2] Solomon's wisdom is remembered because it is preserved in the record of God's holy Scripture; but how short-lived is human fame, seeing that men, in their day the wisest in the East, but for this verse would be altogether forgotten!

Solomon's wealth and power was much increased by the aid of several flourishing cities which had arisen upon the coasts of his kingdom. We read, in the book of Judges, that a portion of the nations of Canaan was left "to prove Israel, whether they would hearken unto the commandments of the Lord."[3] The chief which are mentioned are the Philistines, who occupied their south-western, and the Sidonians, who lived upon their north-western, boundary. These tribes were known among the Greeks by the general title of Phœnicians. The Philistines had already tried Israel by war; and David had been raised up as the great deliverer who finally prevailed over their assaults. Henceforth the Sidonians were to tempt them by the arts of peace; and their evil example had a great share in effecting Israel's downfall.

The Sidonians were, indeed, at times at war with Israel; and, as was their custom whenever they could seize captives,

[1] B.C. 1015. [2] 1 Kings iv. 31. [3] Judg. iii. 4.

they "sold the children of Israel and the children of Jerusalem unto the Grecians;"[1] but in general peace existed between them,—a thing the more necessary to the Sidonians, because, as in after-years, "their country was nourished by" the land of Israel.[2] For already "Judah, and the land of Israel, traded in their market wheat of Minnith, and honey, and oil, and balm."[3] This friendly connexion was strengthened by the tie of a common language. Though the Sidonians were children of Ham, yet their country, one of the earliest peopled in the world ("Hebron was built seven years before Zoan in the land of Egypt,"[4]) was no doubt inhabited before the confusion of tongues; and either from this circumstance, or from subsequent intercourse, their language was the same with that of their Jewish neighbours.[5]

Thus undisturbed on the side of the continent, the Phœnicians had built several powerful cities upon peninsulas or small islands adjoining to the northern shore of the land of Israel. The most northerly of these, Aradus, was considerably beyond their boundary: it stood upon an island; and opposite to it was another town on the continent, called from its position Antaradus. The next towards the south was Tripolis, which still exists. Then came Byblus, or Berytus, now Beyroot. Southward of Berytus lay Sidon, the first of these Phœnician cities which stood properly upon Israelitish ground. But southward still, within the limits of the tribe of Asher, lay Tyre, the last and chiefest of all their cities, a Sidonian colony, as early as the time of Joshua;[6] originally built upon a peninsula, but afterwards

---

[1] Joel iii. 6; Amos i. 9. [2] Acts xii. 20.
[3] Ezek. xxvii. 17. [4] Num. xiii. 22.

[5] To give a single instance: in Carthage, a Tyrian colony, the ruling officers were called *suffetes*; evidently the same word with the Jewish name of the judges, *shophetim*.

[6] Josephus supposes it to have been founded during the times of the Judges; but the account given by Herodotus (ii. 44) accords with the book of Joshua (xix. 29).

transferred to an island about half a mile from the shore; and so small (only twenty-two furlongs in circumference),[1] that its inhabitants were compelled to raise their houses to an unusual height.

These five cities, but especially the last two, had attained in the time of Solomon to an unparalleled greatness; engrossing all the trade which at that time existed in the world. There was then no nation which possessed any power except the Assyrians and Egyptians, with both of whom the Phœnicians carried on a gainful traffic.[2] But their greatest power was derived from the colonies which they settled on the various barbarian coasts which their ships visited. They had penetrated into the Black Sea, where they had founded the city of Bithynium: of "Tubal and Meshech," the Tibareni and Moschi, who inhabited Georgia, they purchased the "persons of men;" while Togarmah, or Cappadocia, "traded in their fairs with mules and horses."[3] The inhabitants of Greece and Italy were a people destined, in their time, to play a higher part in the world's history; and there the Phœnicians were unable to make any permanent settlements, though a few of their emigrants mingled with the Greeks, and they carried off from its coast a few prisoners; but along the other shores of the Mediterranean they spread without opposition. Their most important colonies were on the northern coast of Africa, Utica, Carthage, Adrumetum; but they are said also to have settled on the western margin of Africa, along the shore of the Atlantic, and to have gone northward as far as Britain and the Baltic.[4] They occupied, likewise, the islands of the Mediterranean, Cyprus or Chittim, Sicily, and the Balearic Isles. These stations they had taken with a view to their trade with the most important of all their subject countries, Tarshish or Tartessus, the country at the

---

[1] Pliny, v. 17. Strabo, xvi. 757. [2] Herodotus, i. 1.
[3] Ezek. xxvii. 13, 14. Bochart, "Peleg," iii. 11, 12.
[4] Heeren, "Ideen," i. § 2, p. 53.

mouth of the Guadalquiver in Spain. Spain was at that time rich in minerals; "by reason of the multitude of all kinds of riches, with silver, iron, tin, and lead, she traded in the fairs" of Tyre.[1] Strabo mentions that in the south of Spain there were two hundred places of Phœnician origin; and the people of the country were subjected by them to the same oppression, in searching for the precious metals, to which they themselves afterwards subjected the Indians of America. "Flow freely through thy land, like the Nile, O daughter of Tarshish,"[2] the prophet exclaims on the destruction of Tyre; "for no bond restrains thee any more."[3]

Such was the traffic of the Phœnicians with the West; and they were now united in the closest alliance with the kingdom of Solomon, which afforded equal advantages for what was of no less importance—their trade with the East. Their cities were the great marts for spices and gold from the south of Arabia; and for ebony, ivory, and cotton from the nearer part of India. This trade had hitherto been carried on principally by caravans with Haran, Canna, Aden, and Saba,[4] places at the south-west of Arabia, which still retain the same names. Another mode of communication was with the town of Gerra, near the Persian Gulf. Here the Phœnicians had a colony in the small island of Dedan, a name given by Ezekiel to two places—one a town in the north of Arabia,[5] which supplied the Tyrians with wool by the produce of its flocks; the other a mart where the wealth of India was collected.[6] "The men of Dedan were thy merchants; many isles were the merchandise of thine hand: they brought thee for presents horns of ivory

---

[1] Ezek. xxvii. 12.

[2] From the size of the vessels required for this voyage, the Jews called large ships "a navy of Tarshish," 1 Kings x. 22.

[3] Is. xxiii. 10, according to Gesenius's translation.

[4] Ez. xxvii. 23; and Heeren, i. § 2, p. 102.

[5] Ez. xxvii. 20.   [6] Bochart, "Peleg," iv. 6.

and ebony."[1] The caravans from this quarter came directly across the peninsula of Arabia; and the disturbances in that country are described, therefore, as disturbing them in their course: "In the wilds of Arabia do ye lodge, ye caravans of Dedan. The inhabitants of the land of Teman [in the central part of Arabia] bring water to him that is thirsty, they come with bread to meet the fugitive. For they fly from the sword."[2] The importance of the town of Petra in Edom, of which great remains still exist, was derived from its being the depôt of their traffic. It occupies a hollow pass in a valley, surrounded by inaccessible rocks; and in it, as Diodorus[3] assures us, the Arabians used to hold a common mart of their merchandise. From Petra the merchandise of the East was carried to what Herodotus calls "the Arabian marts,"[4] in the neighbourhood of Gaza, and thus was conveyed by sea to Tyre.

But the conquests of Solomon opened a new and better channel for their commerce. By reducing Edom, and establishing his authority through the country to the north of the Red Sea, he was able to open the harbours of Eloth and Ezion Geber to Phœnician enterprise. The united fleets of Solomon and of Hiram, king of Tyre, visited Ophir a name given to the shores of the southern ocean beyond the Red Sea and Persian Gulf. The coasting voyage down the Red Sea was then so difficult, that a year was spent by these vessels in their progress and return, and an intervening year in the collection of their cargo.[5]

Solomon likewise facilitated the commerce of the Tyrians by building two "store-cities,"[6] Baalath or Balbec, and "Tadmor," or Palmyra, "in the wilderness."[7] Palmyra especially, upon an oasis in the great desert between Tyre and Babylon, three days' journey from the Euphrates, was of much service to the caravans which passed to that

[1] Ez. xxvii. 15.   [2] Is. xxi. 13-15.   [3] Book xix. 6.
[4] Herodotus, iii. 6.   [5] 1 Kings x. 22.   [6] Heeren, i. § 2. p. 125
[7] 1 Kings ix. 18.

place, the great central emporium of the East. By thus contributing to the traffic of Tyre, Solomon shared in its wealth; so that he "made silver to be in Jerusalem as stones, and cedars made he to be as sycamore-trees that are in the vale for abundance."[1] And certainly he turned his wealth to the noblest purpose to which human riches can be made subservient. He made his connexion with the Phœnician cities the means of rearing that majestic temple for God's service, which had been designed by David his father, but which was not to be built save by a man of peace. He perceived that the true end of human greatness was to consecrate of his best to this purpose. "The house that is to be builded," David had said, "must be very magnifical, of fame and of glory throughout all countries;"[2] "for the palace is not for man, but for the Lord God." "But who am I, and what is my people, that we should be able to offer so willingly after this sort? for all things come of Thee, and of Thine own have we given Thee."[3]

In this spirit did Solomon raise a fixed habitation for God's service.

The Tabernacle of the congregation, a tent which Moses had been ordered to set up in the wilderness, had been the place in which God's glory had hitherto been displayed. It had two chambers—an outer and an inner, or most holy place. In this last the ark was placed, and over it was the mercy-seat, where God vouchsafed to manifest His presence in a cloud and flame. As it is the privilege of the Christian Church that our Lord is more especially present in its congregations, so was it the glory of Israel that in its place of national worship God appeared. But in the time of Samuel the ark had been removed from Shiloh; and after being restored by the Philistines, who had taken it captive, it had been kept in various places till David brought it to Mount Sion. There Solomon finally placed it, in the most

---

[1] 1 Kings x. 27.　　[2] 1 Chron. xxii. 5.　　[3] 1 Chron. xxix. 1, 14.

Israel: Its Judges, Prophets, and Kings. 37

holy place of his temple, which became from that time the centre of Israel's worship.

But though Solomon employed his wealth for so noble a purpose, yet his great riches, and his connexion with the surrounding heathen, led, even in his time, to a baneful result. "His wives turned away his heart," and "he went after Ashtoreth, the goddess of the Zidonians."[1] It seemed as though the perfect development of human society could not safely blend with the Church of God till the races of men had gone through their course, and the sons of Japheth should have taken up their final dwelling in the tents of Shem. Meanwhile this union with the sons of Ham, though natural, and though consecrated to higher purposes, was not without its evil. And since prosperity and peace could not remain when innocence had departed, therefore civil commotion and discontent overcast, like a dark cloud, the evening of the life of Solomon.

So incomplete were those preparatory fulfilments of prophecy which led the way for its complete accomplishment in the Church of Christ. In Solomon one part of the promise to Abraham seems for a time to be satisfied; yet is his glory diminished before his death, as though to prove that the kingdom of Israel is not yet completely manifested. David has the assurance of eternal dominion; yet the kingdom of peace is not to be looked for in his days. Moses, the lawgiver, may not enter the land of promise. Only in the Son of God do these separate characters find their complete perfection. For "the likeness of the promised Mediator is conspicuous throughout the sacred volume as in a picture, moving along the line of the history in one or other of His destined offices; the dispenser of blessings in Joseph—the inspired interpreter of truth in Moses—the conqueror in Joshua—the active preacher in

---

[1] 1 Kings xi. 5.

Samuel—the suffering combatant in David—and in Solomon the triumphant and glorious king."[1]

ISRAEL AND JUDAH.

Jeroboam—New Mode of Worship—Ahab—Elijah—Captivity of Israel—Election Passes to Judah.

B.C. 975.

"Those things which are here set down, abridged from the sacred volumes, are not presented to the reader that he may neglect the source from which they come, but rather that his familiar knowledge of the Scripture may enable him to recognise what here he reads; for from the fountain-head alone can be drawn the full mysteries of divine truth."—SULPICIUS SEVERUS, i. § 1.

ON the death of Solomon the kingdom of Israel was divided. That such should be the case had been predicted by God as a punishment for Solomon's sins; it

---

[1] Newman's "History of the Arians," i. § 3.

[It appears that the foundation and growth of the Hebrew monarchy was contemporaneous with the rise in Egypt of the twenty-first dynasty, which began in the person of the Theban priest Hirhor. Internal dissensions and disunion rendered Egypt powerless to check the development of the Hebrew power. Shishak, who founded the twenty-second dynasty, having overthrown that of the Theban usurper, afforded a refuge to Jeroboam; and very possibly then formed some alliance with him, which strengthened him in his operations against Rehoboam. Up to the time of the growth of Hebrew national spirit under Saul, and David, and the zenith of the monarchy under Solomon, who closely allied himself with the Phœnician commercial power upon the coast, the power of Egypt had been much felt in Syria. The division of the kingdom was the signal for the recommencement of Egyptian interference; and in the fifth year of Rehoboam Shishak attacked Jerusalem, and reduced and plundered it (1 Kings xiv. 25 *et* 55). There is a monumental record of this expedition upon the walls of the temple of Ammon at Thebes.—ED.]

was brought about by the folly of Rehoboam, Solomon's son, and by the turbulence of the people. Two tribes only, Judah and Benjamin, remained subject to Rehoboam; the other ten made Jeroboam, the son of Nebat, their king. Now, since the blessing of Abraham had been expressly confined to the line of David's seed, and his descendants were to be kings for ever, this separation from his family was not only a rebellion against their natural prince, but also an abandonment of that religious hope which was the heritage of their nation. This was felt by Jeroboam, who, fearing lest the blessings and hopes of the temple-worship should carry back his people to their former sovereign, resolved to alter the old religion. He began by depriving the priests and Levites of the office, which they had by inheritance, of being God's ministers, and setting up in their rooms priests of his own.[1] They had exercised their office by succession from the time of Aaron; but Jeroboam "made priests of the lowest of the people, which were not of the sons of Levi."[2] How could such men's sacrifices be accepted, any more than those of Dathan and Abiram in the wilderness? They were destitute of the only circumstance which could give authority to any new line of ministers—such power of working miracles as proved them to have received a commission from God. This was not needed by the Jewish priests, because they inherited that authority from Aaron, which had at first been approved by supernatural tokens. Yet it pleased God to give a sign of the futility of Jeroboam's plans, and to accompany it by a lesson which indicated their danger. A prophet was sent from Judah, and at his word Jeroboam's altar was rent, its ashes poured out, and his own hand subsequently withered.[3] This prophet had received God's direct injunction not to eat or drink in Jeroboam's dominions, nor to return by the way by which he went. He listened, however, to the words of another pretended prophet, who professed to have a

---

[1] 2 Chron. xi. 13. [2] 1 Kings xii. 31. [3] 1 Kings xiii.

message from God by which his own was superseded. Though himself guided by an inspiration which God had avouched by miracle, he rested and ate, trusting to the assurances of a person who gave no such sign of the reality of his mission. For such irreverence God was pleased to sentence him to death: " a lion met him and slew him." And in his history Jeroboam might see a reflection of his own impiety, in substituting a line of priests by his own authority, for those, the origin of whose succession had been sanctioned by the supernatural power of God.

With a new set of priests Jeroboam set up a new mode of worship. The people had been wont, according to God's command, to go up three times a-year to worship at Jerusalem. But Jeroboam set up two golden calves at the two ends of his kingdom, at Bethel and Dan, and persuaded the people to regard them as signs of the Being whom they had been wont to serve : " Behold thy gods, O Israel, which brought thee up out of the land of Egypt."[1] Thus did he corrupt God's worship for the sake of preserving his power ; but he did so to his own injury. Even after God had warned him by a prophet, " he returned not from his evil way, but made again of the lowest of the people priests of the high places; whoever would, he consecrated him, and he became one of the priests of the high places. And this thing became sin unto the house of Jeroboam, even to cut it off, and to destroy it from off the face of the earth."

After Jeroboam and his son, various kings ruled over the ten tribes; but they continued to worship those calves which had been designed to draw men from God's temple at Jerusalem. At length, about fifty years after Jeroboam's time,* Ahab introduced the worship of Baal from the

[1] 1 Kings xii. 28.

* Ahab's alliance with the Sidonian and other Syrian States is illustrated by the Assyrian monumental inscriptions. His name is found amongst those who formed the confederation against which Shalmanezar III. conducted his first campaign in B.C. 853; other contingents were those from Hamath, Damascus, Egypt, and Arabia. These were

neighbouring city of Sidon. This he did at the persuasion of his wife Jezebel, the daughter of the king of Sidon; and so besotted was she by this idol-worship, that she sought to slay all the prophets or teachers of the true religion who remained in the land of Israel. But at this time God raised up Elijah the Tishbite to be a restorer of His service, and gave him such courage, power, and influence, that he became the founder of a new line of prophets in Israel, and prevented the true faith from being totally lost. He began by praying for a great drought, which God sent in answer to his prayers.[1] It was a painful thing to witness the want and misery which this drought occasioned throughout the whole country; but better it was that they should suffer this affliction than that God's favour should be for ever lost to the nation.[2] At a later period God sent down fire from heaven upon the altar which Elijah had built upon Mount Carmel; and the whole nation, which was looking on, confessed, "The Lord, He is the God; the Lord, He is the God."[3] Thus commissioned, Elijah put to death the priests of Baal, according to the law of Moses; he predicted Ahab's own destruction and that of his family, and the Lord "let none of his words fall to the ground." He, too, was a type of Christ in his afflictions, as in his spirit and power of John the Baptist;[4] and as Moses had done before him, he fasted

---

defeated at the battle of Karkar. Some confusion of date for a time made this rather doubtful; but the Assyrian inscriptions are throughout consistent with themselves, and demonstrate that an error of about forty years has crept into the chronological system adopted in the Bible margins. The result of the battle of Karkar was the breaking up of the Syrian league; and perhaps this accounts for the alliance which in the latter period of his reign Ahab appears to have formed with the kingdom of Judah. This same Shalmanezar has left on record the payment of tribute (as the result of a later Syrian expedition in the year 842 B.C.), by Jehu the "son of Omri"—"Yahua abil Khumri;" he does not appear to have been aware of the revolution in Samaria by which Jehu obtained the throne.

[1] James v. 17. [2] 1 Kings xviii. 17. [3] 1 Kings xviii. 39.
[4] Luke i. 17; 1 Kings xix. 8.

forty days in the wilderness, where his great Master was to undergo the like trial.[1] By Elijah, and Elisha who came after him, schools of the sons of the prophets were set up or strengthened, which served to maintain some measure of piety in the land. Yet all things went back, as might have been expected when the promise of Abraham was despised; so that at length the nation of Israel was carried captive into the land of Assyria, never to be reinstated. "For so it was, that the children of Israel had sinned against the Lord their God, which had brought them up out of the land of Egypt, and had feared other gods, and walked in the statutes of the heathen. And the children of Israel did secretly those things that were not right against the Lord their God, and they built them high places in all their cities, from the tower of the watchman to the fenced city. And they set them up images and groves in every high hill, and under every green tree. And there they burnt incense in all the high places, as did the heathen whom the Lord carried away before them; and wrought wicked things to provoke the Lord to anger. For they served idols, whereof the Lord had said unto them, Ye shall not do this thing. Yet the Lord testified against Israel, and against Judah, by all the prophets, and by all the seers, saying, Turn ye from your evil ways, and keep My commandments and My statutes. Notwithstanding they would not hear, but hardened their necks, like to the neck of their fathers, that did not believe in the Lord their God. And they left all the commandments of the Lord their God, and made them molten images, even two calves, and made a grove, and worshipped all the host of heaven, and served Baal. And they caused their sons and their daughters to pass through the fire, and used divination and enchantments, and sold themselves to do evil in the sight of the Lord, to provoke Him to anger. Therefore the Lord was very angry with Israel, and removed them out of His sight; there was none

---

[1] 2 Kings vi. 1.

Israel and Judah.

left but the tribe of Judah only. And the Lord rejected all the seed of Israel, and afflicted them, and delivered them into the hand of the spoilers, until He had cast them out of His sight. So was Israel carried out of their own land into Assyria unto this day."[1]

Meanwhile the kingdom of Judah was prosperous when it served God, and afflicted when it forsook Him. Yet as its kings continued to be that line of David to which God's ancient promise was secured, and as the public worship of the temple and ordinances of the law were not interrupted, the nation still remained God's people, though its many sins brought heavy punishments. When it walked in the statutes of Israel, it shared for the time in Israel's punishment. But the public actions of the nation depended much upon its prince; and though some of the kings of Judah, as Ahaziah and Ahaz, were wicked, some were good, as Asa, Jehoshaphat, and Hezekiah. This last was on the throne of Judah when the ten[*] tribes were finally cast off, and carried captive into Assyria. And then it was that God declared by His prophet Hosea, that His election, which had fallen on Isaac, one of the sons of Abraham, and on Jacob, instead of his brother Esau, should move henceforth in the line of the Jewish nation. "Ephraim compasseth Me about with lies, and the house of Israel with deceit; but Judah yet ruleth with God, and is faithful with the saints."[2]

---

[1] 2 Kings xvii. 7, &c.   [2] Hosea xi. 12.

[*] In B.C. 722, Sargon, the commander in chief under Shalmanezar IV., captured the Israelite capital; and in his inscriptions at Khorsabad the events are thus narrated—

"I besieged, I occupied the city of Samaria, and I carried away 27,230 of the inhabitants. I took . . . 50 chariots; I carried them away to Assyria, and in their places put men whom my hand had conquered; I appointed my officers as prefects over them."

It would therefore appear that it was a portion, and not the whole of the ten tribes that was at this time carried into captivity. There was a renewed outbreak, however, a few years later.

ASSYRIAN EMPIRE RESTORED.

Hezekiah — Isaiah — Prophets — Chaldees — Babylon — Its Commerce and Splendour — Captivity of Judah — Tyre — Apries — Prophecy of the Five Empires.

B.C. 747.

"Prophecy is but Divine history, which hath that prerogative over human, as the narration may be before the fact."

LORD BACON.

AFTER the death of Sardanapalus the Assyrian empire was divided for a time into two parts, one of which had for its capital Babylon, and Nineveh the other. By this last, which had the easier communication with Canaan, the ten tribes were carried into captivity. Ten years* later,[1] Sennacherib, who had succeeded Shalmanezar, came up against Judah. At this time the kingdom of Babylon was little dreaded, for the wide desert seemed to be an effectual barrier between it and Jerusalem. And therefore, when its king sent messengers to congratulate Hezekiah on his recovery from sickness, he told the prophet Isaiah that they came "from a far country, even from Babylon."[2] But this

---

[1] B.C. 721.   [2] Isaiah xxxix. 6.

* Shalmanezar IV. was succeeded by Sargon: upon his death, B.C. 705, Sennacherib succeeded him. During the absence of Sargon, Merodach Baladan obtained the throne of Babylon. The mission to Hezekiah was sent by him, with the object, very possibly, of engaging Sargon against him, and diverting him from his object of reducing the Babylonian kingdom. A terra-cotta cylinder, discovered by Mr George Smith, of the *Daily Telegraph* expedition, gives an account of a conquest of Judea by Sargon in B.C. 711. This adventure, previously unknown, corresponds very accurately with the 10th and 11th chapters of Isaiah. After this unrecorded siege of Jerusalem, Sargon returned to Babylon, and overcame Merodach Baladan; and left to Sennacherib, his son, upon his death, a united empire. In B.C. 701 Sennacherib undertook a new expedition against Syria, received the submission of the kings of Ashdod, Ammon, Moab, and Edom, and took captive the kings of Ashkelon and Ekron, which held out against him for a time.

Assyrian Empire Restored. 45

distant and friendly kingdom was declared by God to be appointed for the final punishment of the Jewish people, while from their more threatening enemies of Nineveh they were miraculously delivered. When Sennacherib was already encamped against Jerusalem, "the angel of the Lord went forth, and smote in the camp of the Assyrians a hundred and four score and five thousand."[1] The promise of present preservation, and the assurance that the nation most dreaded was not appointed to injure them, gave peace and tranquillity during the remnant of Hezekiah's days; and at this time[2] God bestowed upon His people a still further

---

[1] Isaiah xxxvii. 36.   [2] B.C. 710.

The "Taylor" cylinder in the British Museum gives an account of this expedition. It concludes with the following account, which appears to imply that he was also successful against Hezekiah at the same time:—
"But as for Hezekiah, king of Judah, who had not submitted to my yoke, forty-six of his strong cities, together with innumerable fortresses, and small towns which depended upon them, by overthrowing the walls, by attack and battle, with engines and battering-rams I besieged, I captured. I brought out from the midst of them, and counted as spoil, 200,150 persons, small and great, male and female, horses, mules, asses, camels, oxen, and sheep without number; Hezekiah himself I shut up like a bird in a cage in Jerusalem, his royal city. I built a line of forts against him, and kept his foot from going forth from the gate of his city. I cut off his city, which I had spoiled, from the midst of his land, and gave them to Metaite, king of Ashdod, and Padia, king of Ekron, and Yil-ball, king of Gaza, and I reduced his country. In addition to the former tribute and gifts I levied more tribute, and the homage due to my Majesty I laid upon him. The fear of the greatness of my Majesty overwhelmed him, even he himself; and he sent after me to Nineveh, my royal city, gifts and tribute, the mercenaries and his bodyguard whom he had brought for the defence of Jerusalem, his royal city, and furnished with pay, together with thirty talents of gold, 800 talents of silver, bright and fresh as stones, a couch of ivory, elephants' hides, elephants' tusks, rare woods of every kind, a vast treasure, as well as the eunuchs of his palace, singing men and singing women; and he sent his ambassadors to offer homage."

This boastful account contains an important confirmation, however, of the truth of the Bible narrative; for it is clear that for some reason he was obliged to raise the siege of Jerusalem, and quoted the present

blessing in those predictions of the final glories of Christ's kingdom, which form the last half of Isaiah's prophecy. The first half of this book refers, for the most part, to God's judgments on the Jews and the surrounding nations; the last part of it, to their deliverance from captivity, and to the coming of the Saviour, which lay beyond. And these predictions it pleased God to give in a tranquil period of His Church's history, as though their character of thanksgiving and confidence was to agree with the peaceful and prosperous state of the period when they were given. Their very style and language is calm, easy, and flowing, and differs much from the abrupt and passionate sentences in which God's judgments upon His sinful people are predicted.

It was not until four generations after Hezekiah, that Isaiah's predictions concerning Babylon were accomplished. Manasseh, Hezekiah's son, had especially provoked God's wrath against His people, by filling Jerusalem with the innocent blood of His servants.[1] No national sin so much excited God's anger as this persecution of His Church. In it Isaiah is supposed to have perished,—sawn asunder by Manasseh's order.[2] This was the age of the chief prophets. Jeremiah's predictions were uttered in the time of Josiah, Manasseh's grandson, and of Josiah's sons. In the latter part of this time, Ezekiel prophesied in Chaldæa, and Daniel in Babylon. Hosea and Micah had lived in the days of Hezekiah; Amos shortly before. Thus was the Jewish Church prepared for that great judgment which was shortly to fall upon it. The CAPTIVITY,—delayed for a time in consequence of Josiah's reformation,—came shortly afterwards, in the days of Zedekiah, Josiah's son.

[1] 2 Kings xxiv. 4.   [2] Heb. xi. 37.
which Hezekiah had sent to him at Lachish (2 Kings xviii. 14) as a tribute wrested from him by a victory he had not achieved—as a matter of fact he never, during his lifetime, invaded Syria again, which is conclusive evidence that his former attempt had failed, however glowing the story of success he dressed up for the satisfaction of his people.

Assyrian Empire Restored. 47

Babylon* had by this time attained that dangerous greatness which Isaiah had predicted, when the ambassadors of its king Merodach Baladan had visited Hezekiah. The independence of Babylon had at that time been short; for when Merodach Baladan had reigned for half a year, Sennacherib conquered him, and established his son Esarhaddon upon the throne. But in the interval which had since elapsed a new power had grown up in Asia.[1] The Chaldæans, a people of Japhetic race,[2] whose native land was the mountainous region to the north of Assyria, where they were still found in the time of Cyrus,[3] whether introduced as mercenaries by their less hardy neighbours, or by whatever means they were settled in the neighbourhood of Babylon, had now become its masters. "This people was not," says the prophet,[4] "till the Assyrian founded it for them that dwell in the wilderness." But "when the Assyrian power was beginning to sink, the Chaldæans in Babylon united themselves to other tribes which were preparing to revolt, and, under the guidance of their conquering chief Nebuchadnezzar, played the part of their former lords."[5] Babylon, therefore, was the great seat of their strength, "the beauty of the Chaldees' excellency;"[6] and it was especially under "Nebuchadnezzar the Chaldæan,"[7] that it became "the glory of kingdoms," "the golden city."[8]

How it came to this measure of greatness, and what was the peculiar feature which led Daniel afterwards to describe it as a "head of gold," shall now be mentioned. Till the improvements in navigation opened a passage to the East Indies by the Cape of Good Hope, the Persian Gulf was the great channel through which all traffic from the East flowed into the western world. It has been mentioned that

---

[1] *Vide* the Armenian edition of Eusebius's "Chronicon," in Gesenius on Is. xxxix. 1.
[2] Gesenius, p. 748. [3] Cyrop. iii. 2, § 7, 12.
[4] Is. xxiii. 13.   [5] Gesenius on Is. xxiii. 13, p. 747.
[6] Is. xiii. 19.   [7] Ezra v. 12.   [8] Is. xiv. 4.
* With reference to this passage, see preceding note.

the merchants of Dedanim carried their wares across Arabia to Tyre. But Babylon lay in the most favourable position to engross this traffic; ships could sail to her up the Euphrates from the Indian Sea; and hence, at an early period, she had become the centre of trade in that part of the East. To this day Bagdad and the adjoining cities upon the Euphrates present a singular contrast in wealth and manners to the wild mountains of Persia on the south-east of them. "Though but a shadow of what it was, Bagdad is still the caravansera of Asia."[1] And in ancient times Babylon was "a land of traffic, a city of merchants."[2] Hence Isaiah speaks of "the Chaldæans, whose cry is in the ships;" and Æschylus tells of "the mingled crowd sent forth by the wealthy Babylon, archers and managers of vessels."[3]

Herodotus, an eye-witness of the magnificence of Babylon, gives us some account of the trade with which its river supplied it. He speaks especially of that with Armenia and Mesopotamia, whence vast quantities of the necessaries of life were brought in large coracles, some of them five thousand talents in burthen, formed of ribs of wood overlaid with a covering of hides.[4] When these vessels arrived at Babylon their frameworks were broken up and sold, while the hides were carried home upon the back of an ass, which was brought down in the vessel.

In this manner the city was supported. But its wealth was derived from vessels which came to it immediately from the sea, or landed their cargoes at Gerra, its colony on the Persian Gulf.[5] This traffic had probably diminished in the time of Herodotus, since it was discouraged by the Persian conquerors of Babylon. But it was thus that the Babylonians were supplied with cotton, which they wove into those garments of which we hear as early as the days of Joshua.[6]

---

[1] Porter; quoted by Heeren, "Ideen," i. § 2, p. 200.
[2] Ezek. xvii. 4.   [3] Persæ, 52.
[4] Herod. i. 194.   [5] Heeren, i. § 2, p. 232.
[6] Josh. vii. 21; Herod. i. 195.

From the Persian Gulf, also, they received pearls, bamboos, and gems, which they were celebrated for their skill in cutting.[1] Cinnamon they imported from the Isle of Ceylon —"the sweet cane," which came, as Jeremiah tells us, "from a far country."[2]

But besides this seafaring activity, which had its common effect in corrupting their manners, and bringing them, as Herodotus assures us,[3] to an unusual measure of immodesty, Babylon was likewise the great depôt for trade with the further part of India, with which the ancients communicated by land. Thus from that portion of India, which was afterwards part of the Persian empire, near the sources of the Indus, they received cochineal.[4] There was considerable traffic with Lesser Thibet, along a road which, passing from Assyria through the Caspian Straits, a celebrated pass near the south of the Caspian Sea, afterwards led on to Bactria and Aria. These countries bordered on the tribes which are called by Herodotus the northern Indians, of whom he speaks as supplying vast quantities of gold-dust, which they procured from ant-hills in the great desert of Kobi.[5] His account evidently shews that great riches were procured from that quarter; and also that those from whom he derived his information were unwilling to reveal the method in which it was procured. But Ctesias tells us, that when the Indians went on the expeditions in which they procured gold, it was in large bodies; and that their journey lasted for three or four years.[6] So that we seem to discover that the trade by which Babylon was enriched was carried on through the medium of caravans with the most distant parts of the East.

At the time of its great prosperity, and either by Nebu-

---

[1] Heeren, i. § 2, p. 246; and Herod. i. 195. [2] Jer. vi. 20.
[3] Herod. i. 199. [4] Ctesias, in Heeren's "Ideen," i. 2. p. 214.
[5] Herod. vii. 102.
[6] Ctesias, in Heeren, "Ideen," i. 2. p. 219.

chadnezzar or his queen, Babylon was adorned with public works of the most gigantic kind. The city was built in a vast square on each side of the river Euphrates; its whole circuit being fifty-four miles.[1] Each front was thirteen and a half miles in length; its walls were nearly three hundred and fifty feet high; its streets were parallel to one another; and it had one hundred brazen gates. Brazen gates, likewise, and a flanking wall, secured each division of the city from the river. They were joined by a wooden bridge,[2] which was removed at night, and was supported by a stone pier in the midst of the river. In the centre of the eastern division stood the palace; the temple of Belus on the western side was the magnificent tower, consisting of eight stages raised one upon another,[3] which gave name to the place. The ruins of this pile remain—a confused mass of earth and masonry—and are still called by the wandering Arabs Birs Nimrod, or Nimrod's Tower.[4] On the other side of the river, in the neighbourhood of the palace, was a work almost as remarkable,—a garden formed of immense terraces, reared upon solid masonry; a work which Nebuchadnezzar is said to have reared for his queen, who, "being a native of the hilly country of Media, was accustomed to such a prospect."[5]

Such was the internal appearance of a city which was at this time raised up to be the head of the East. After uniting all the ancient power of the Assyrian empire, Nebuchadnezzar defeated Pharaoh-Necho at Circesium[6] (on the Euphrates), and drove the Egyptians altogether out of Asia. The power of the Egyptians, the only rivals of Assyria, being thus broken, he overspread the East with his armies. He shut up the Tyrians within their walls, and besieged

---

[1] Herod. i. 179-181.
[2] Herod. i. 186.
[3] Herod. i. 181.
[4] Heeren, "Ideen," i. § 2, p. 170.
[5] Josephus contra Apion, i.
[6] Jer. xlvi. 2. B.C. 604.

them for thirteen years.[1] At this time they appear to have removed to the island,[2] which hence became Tyre; for when attacked by Alexander, at a later period, we read of no attempt to defend their ancient fortifications. After the capture or destruction of old Tyre, Nebuchadnezzar marched into Egypt. Apries, or Pharaoh-Hophra, the grandson of Necho,[3] who then was king, had hitherto been successful in his enterprises; and such was his confidence, that he had been wont to boast that "the gods themselves could not deprive him of his power."[4] His pride had provoked the anger of Jehovah, who declared by the mouth of Ezekiel, "Behold, I am against thee, Pharaoh king of Egypt, the great dragon that lieth in the midst of his rivers, which hath said, My river is mine own, and I have made it for myself."[5] Nebuchadnezzar was chosen to execute God's sentence:[6] he speedily overran and plundered Egypt,[7] and inflicted upon it a blow from which it did not shortly recover.[8]

By this conquering prince the sins of God's own people were to be punished. He was led against them shortly after his accession to the throne; he burnt the city[9] and the glorious temple which Solomon had built; and, according to the common policy at that period of removing conquered nations, with a view of breaking up the associations which connected them with their former state, he carried the people captive to Babylon. Thus was fulfilled

[1] Josephus contra Apion, i.

[2] It is stated, on the one hand, that Nebuchadnezzar should not have the spoil of Tyre (Ez. xxix. 18); yet on the other, that he should destroy its walls (Ez. xxvi. 10).

[3] *Vide* p. 23.   [4] Herod. ii. 169.   [5] Ez. xxiv. 3.

[6] Herodotus takes no notice of this conquest of Egypt; but it is mentioned by Josephus ("Antiquities," x. 11), who cites Megasthenes; and Herodotus appears to have received his intelligence solely from the Egyptians themselves, for he mentions Necho's victory over the Jews, but not his defeat at Carchemish, which is necessary to explain his retreat.

[7] B.C. 571.   [8] Ez. xxix. 13.   [9] B.C. 587.

Isaiah's prophecy, and thus was the Church punished by being subjected for a season to that worldly empire over which it was finally to prevail.

The first, therefore, of the four monarchies had now reached its height. Its capital, Babylon, was the greatest as well as most ancient city in the world. The most civilised and best-peopled portions of the earth were subject to it. The heirs of that divine promise, which has bound together the most distant parts of the world, were swallowed up for a time in its greatness. But just at this season, He who has given bounds to the great deep was pleased to declare what should be the limits to man's ambition, and where its proud waves should be stayed. At the very moment when the first empire had reached its greatness, and when it touched upon that humble polity of Israel, which its breath seemed enough to sweep away, God declared the vanity of earthly greatness, and the eternal endurance of His people.

The prophecy of the latter days was given when the spiritual and temporal seed came thus in contact with one another. The concurrence of both was needed to give expression to God's decree, as the union of both was needed to fulfil it. It seemed, therefore, as if another of those great epochs was at hand, when the history of mankind was to be gathered into a single channel. But the union was but for a season. It was not given to the possessors of Nimrod's corrupt kingdom, even though it had fallen into the hands of the more vigorous Chaldæans, to combine permanently with the heirs of promise, and thus to produce between them those great events which were to consummate the fortunes of the world. The office of this first monarchy was but to lead the way; to indicate what should follow. Yet, in order to show how it ministered to the great things of after-times, the temporal power was chosen to receive the vision of what should follow, when its course terminated in the kingdom of Christ. At this place, therefore, the language of Holy Scripture alters, and speaks not in Hebrew, as to the chosen nation, but in the dialect of their Chaldæan conquerors.[1] The king of Babylon himself is chosen to witness to Messiah's power. He consults the wise men of his kingdom, and seeks by their earthly wisdom to interpret his vision. They fail him, and he is driven to that spiritual power with which at this very period he had been brought into connection. Daniel told him, "there is a God in heaven that revealeth secrets, and maketh known to the king Nebuchadnezzar what shall be in the latter days. As for thee, O king, thy thoughts came into thy mind upon thy bed, what should come to pass hereafter: and He that revealeth secrets maketh known to thee what shall come to pass. Thou, O king, sawest, and behold a great image. This great image, whose brightness was excellent, stood before thee; and the form thereof was terrible. This image's head was of fine gold, his breast and his arms of silver, his belly and his thighs of brass, his legs of iron, his feet part of iron and part of clay. Thou sawest till that a stone was cut out without hands, which smote the image upon his feet that were of iron and clay, and brake them to pieces. Then was the iron, the clay, the brass, the silver, and the gold, broken to pieces together, and became like the chaff of the summer threshing-floors; and the wind carried them away, that no place was found for them: and the stone that smote the image became a great mountain, and filled the whole earth. This is the dream, and we will tell the interpretation thereof before the king. Thou, O king, art a king of kings; for the God of heaven hath given thee a kingdom, power, and strength, and glory. And wheresoever the children of men dwell, the beasts of the field and the fowls of the heaven hath He given into thine hand, and hath made thee ruler over them all. Thou art this head of gold. And after thee shall arise another kingdom inferior to thee, and another third kingdom of brass, which shall bear rule

---

[1] Dan. xi. 4, and *infra*.

over all the earth. And the fourth kingdom shall be strong as iron: forasmuch as iron breaketh in pieces and subdueth all things: and as iron that breaketh all these, shall it break in pieces and bruise. And in the days of these kings shall the God of heaven set up a kingdom, which shall never be destroyed: and the kingdom shall not be left to other people, but it shall break in pieces and consume all these kingdoms, and it shall stand for ever. Forasmuch as thou sawest that the stone was cut out of the mountain without hands, and that it brake in pieces the iron, the brass, the clay, the silver, and the gold; the great God hath made known to the king what shall come to pass hereafter: and the dream is certain, and the interpretation thereof sure."[1]

To explain every particular of this prophecy is unnecessary, and perhaps with our present knowledge impossible; but its general purpose cannot be mistaken. We have here the Babylonish empire which then existed, the Persian which followed after, the Grecian which succeeded it, the Roman which was to come last of all. Upon the ruins of the Roman empire Christ's Church was to arise. No other empire was afterwards to exist with that pre-eminence and authority which these four had successively possessed. If others arose, which were equal in actual strength, yet they were not to have the same comparative superiority. No empire after the Roman was to fill the theatre of the world as these did. The great event of following times was to be the establishment of Christ's Church. And so it has happened. There have been great kingdoms in later days; but there has been none which could clearly be said to be chief. These four empires, each in their day, were so. They filled the earth as the chief figure fills a picture, not by occupying the whole, but by leaving space for no figure besides it. So does one sun fill the sky, if not by its actual bulk, yet by the effluence of its beams.

[1] Dan. ii. 28.

Such in their day were the four empires of Babylon, Persia, Greece, and Rome. Such, still more, is the Church of Christ, which was to succeed them. The history of these five kingdoms makes up the history of the world. And this great summary of the fortunes of mankind God was pleased to give just when the first empire had gained its summit of greatness. And, as though to give it greater solemnity and interest, the celebrated king, through whom it was revealed, exhibited in his own person a proof of the true source of power, and was shewn that "the Most High ruleth in the kingdoms of men." Of this he himself published a record for the instruction of the nations.

"I thought it good," he says, "to shew the signs and wonders that the high God hath wrought toward me. How great are His signs, and how mighty are His wonders! His kingdom is an everlasting kingdom, and His dominion is from generation to generation."[1] Nebuchadnezzar then relates how it pleased God when he was at the very pinnacle of greatness, to predict his sudden fall. He might have expected an earthly enemy; but he fell without human hand. "At the end of twelve months he walked in the palace of the kingdom of Babylon. The king spake, and said, Is not this great Babylon, that I have built for the house of the kingdom by the might of my power, and for the honour of my majesty? While the word was in the king's mouth, there fell a voice from heaven, saying, O king Nebuchadnezzar, to thee it is spoken; the kingdom is departed from thee. And they shall drive thee from men, and thy dwelling shall be with the beasts of the field: they shall make thee to eat grass as oxen, and seven times shall pass over thee, until thou know that the most High ruleth in the kingdom of men, and giveth it to whomsoever He will. The same hour was the thing fulfilled upon Nebuchadnezzar: and he was driven from men, and did eat grass as oxen, and his body was wet with the dew of heaven,

[1] Dan. iv. 2.

till his hairs were grown like eagles' feathers, and his nails like birds' claws. And at the end of the days, I, Nebuchadnezzar, lifted up mine eyes unto heaven, and mine understanding returned unto me, and I blessed the most High, and I praised and honoured Him that liveth for ever, whose dominion is an everlasting dominion, and His kingdom is from generation to generation. And all the inhabitants of the earth are reputed as nothing: and He doeth according to His will in the army of heaven, and among the inhabitants of the earth: and none can stay His hand, or say unto Him, What doest Thou? At the same time my reason returned unto me; and for the glory of my kingdom, mine honour and brightness returned unto me; and my counsellors and my lords sought unto me; and I was established in my kingdom, and excellent majesty was added unto me. Now I, Nebuchadnezzar, praise and extol and honour the King of heaven, all whose works are truth, and His ways judgment: and those that walk in pride He is able to abase."

PERSIAN OR SECOND GREAT EMPIRE.

PERSIAN OR SECOND GREAT EMPIRE.

*Cyrus—Crœsus—Oracle at Delphi—Babylon taken—Daniel—
Temple restored—Cambyses—Smerdis the Magian—Darius
Hystaspes—Scythian Expedition.*

> "He look'd, and saw what numbers numberless
> The city-gates outpour'd, light-arm'd troops
> In coats of mail and military pride:
> In mail their horses clad, yet fleet and strong,
> Prancing their riders bore, the flower and choice
> Of many provinces from bound to bound :—
> He saw them in their forms of battle rang'd,
> How quick they wheel'd ; and flying behind them shot
> Sharp steel of arrowy showers against the face
> Of their pursuers, and o'ercame by flight :
> The field, all iron, cast a gleaming brown."
>
> MILTON.

THE Assyrian empire had reached its height under Nebuchadnezzar; it fell with his grandson, Belshazzar.* During the reign of this prince, the Median nation grew powerful, and being assisted by the Persians, it conquered, one by one, most countries of the East. The cavalry of the Medes and Persians was long celebrated as the best, as well as most numerous in the world; and the

* Belshazzar appears to have been the son of Nabonidus, who had been chosen to fill the Babylonian throne by the conspirators who overturned the dynasty of Nabopolassar, and put to death Labossoracus, the grandson of Nebuchadnezzar. It is of course possible that Nabonidus, to confirm himself upon the throne, had married into the family of Nebuchadnezzar, and that Belshazzar was issue of such an alliance. At the time of the fall of Babylon, the inscriptions prove that there was a joint sovereignty of Nabonidus and Belshazzar. Nabonidus, having been defeated by Cyrus, fled to Borsippa; and left the defence of Babylon entirely in the hands of Belshazzar.

corrupted Babylonians were unable to make any successfu head against the vigour and hardihood of these children c Japheth.

Their success must likewise be attributed to the wisdom and courage of Cyrus, prince of Persia. Of his birth and education, many stories are told. Some[1] say that hi grandfather, the king of Media, to whom the Persian were then subject, would have put him to death when a boy, through fear of a dream which predicted his future greatness. A shepherd, who was ordered to destroy him brought him up as his own child; and other boys of hi own age chose him as their leader. When he was known his spirit and appearance won his grandfather's favour and he was raised again to the command which naturally belonged to him. All agree that his childhood gave remarkable promise, which was not disappointed by his age. Him, therefore, God raised up to found the second of those great empires which He had declared should fil the earth. Three times is the extent, nature, and order o this kingdom predicted in the book of Daniel.[2] When the last prediction was given,[3] the Medes and Persians had begun to grow to power; and the prophet declares that the Persians, who were at first the inferior nation, should in the end have the superiority: "I lifted up mine eyes, and saw and, behold, there stood before the river a ram which had two horns: and the two horns were high; but one was higher than the other, and the higher came up last. I saw the ram pushing westward, and northward, and southward so that no beasts might stand before him, neither was there any that could deliver out of his hand; but he did according to his will, and became great."[4]

This superiority of the Persians to their Median neigh bours was not derived from their larger numbers, but from their possessing a greater measure of that courage and good

---

[1] Herod. i. 108, &c.
[3] B.C. 553.
[2] Dan. ii. 39; vii. 5; viii. 3.
[4] Dan. viii. 3, 4.

Persian, or Second Great Empire. 61

conduct in which both these tribes were superior to the other people of the East. Herodotus describes their mode of education even after they had left their own poor and mountainous country: "they teach their children, from the age of five years to that of twenty, these three things—to ride, to shoot with the bow, and to speak the truth."[1] Besides the great contrast which their country exhibited to the enervating plains of the wealthy Babylonians, they had also received a purer system from a remarkable teacher named Zoroaster,[2] who had lived some time before the age of Cyrus. By him they had been taught the folly of that worship of images which was common in the East;[3] and even the errors of his system tended to the increase of their national strength. His opinions were derived from the feeling (not unnatural on an imperfect view of the world), that good and evil were two independent principles, which were striving for the mastery in this state of being. These principles he supposed to be embodied in actually existing beings, attended by their ministering spirits; the good he called *Ormus*, and the bad, *Ahriman*. The empire of the good spirit he supposed to be especially set forth in his own people, whose office, therefore, was to establish a kingdom, in which the principles of excellence might be fully exhibited.[4] Hence his especial attention to agriculture, as being a development of the internal powers of the earth, of which we afterwards see traces in the Persian government.[5] Thus was "the earnest expectation of the creature waiting for the manifestation of the sons of God," and thus were the founders of earthly monarchies anticipating that result which the Church of Christ can alone supply.

It was in this discipline, then, that Cyrus was trained up to be the conqueror of the East. After establishing the

[1] Herod. i. 136. [2] Heeren, "Ideen," i. § 1. p. 440.
[3] Herod. i. 131.
[4] Zendavesta: quoted by Heeren, "Ideen," i. § 1. p. 447.
[5] Heeren, i. § 1. p. 473.

superiority of the Persians over their Median brethren, he reduced the warlike tribes to the north of Assyria, and thus came into contact with Crœsus, king of Lydia, who ruled over the greatest part of Asia Minor.[1] Crœsus had for some time been preparing for the conflict. He had taken the singular course of consulting the oracle at Delphi, which was highly esteemed among the neighbouring states of Greece; having previously tested the reality of its powers. This oracle was supposed to be directed by Apollo, or Pytho as the Greeks called him, the same spirit which the apostle cast forth from the damsel at Philippi.[2] In that case we are assured that the damsel's power of divination was real, because, if merely pretended, her masters would not have lost their hopes of gain; and in like manner the oracle at Delphi at times discovered knowledge which mere human nature could not attain. That such powers are not possessed at present by evil spirits, is no proof that they were not formerly exercised; because the Church is holy ground, and at our Lord's coming, "the prince of the power of the air" "fell from heaven." Crœsus's experiment satisfied him of the wisdom of the oracle at Delphi. He sent messengers from Sardis, his capital, to various oracles, and ordered them on the hundredth day after their departure (so rude was then the mode of estimating time) to enter the consecrated places, where answers were given, and to inquire in what Crœsus, king of Lydia, was at that time employed.[3] Upon the appointed day, he bethought him of what would be the most unlikely occupation in which he could spend his time; and having procured the flesh of a tortoise and mixed it with that of a lamb, he boiled it in a brazen caldron under a brazen lid. Shortly afterwards his messengers returned, having written down the answers which were severally made to them. The others are not recorded; but the messenger who had been sent to Delphi related that he had no sooner proposed his

[1] Xenoph. Cyrop.   [2] Acts xvi. 16 (margin).   [3] Herod. i. 47, 48.

question, than the Pythoness, or woman who gave the answer, replied:—

> "I know the sea and sand's expanse,
> Nor thoughts unuttered 'scape my glance:
> Of tortoise-flesh I scent the smell,
> In boiling cauldron sodden well,
> With weanling of the woolly drove;
> Brass beneath and brass above."

Convinced by this answer of the wisdom of the oracle, Crœsus, after making many rich offerings, consulted it on the result of his war with Cyrus. Its answers shew that if the oracle had some extraordinary power of detecting what was passing at a distance, yet, respecting the future, it could only exercise such sagacity as might delude its votaries, and secure itself from detection. Crœsus was told that if he passed the river Halys—the boundary between himself and the Persians—he should destroy a great empire; and again, that he was secure till a mule sat upon the throne of Media. When, in reliance on these assurances, he had attacked Cyrus,[1] been defeated, and taken prisoner, he was told that the mule was Cyrus, born of a Median and Persian parent, and that the empire which he had overturned was his own."[2]

After the conquest of Lydia, Cyrus turned his arms against Babylon, which the Jewish prophets had so long before declared that he should destroy. Isaiah had marked him out by name as the deliverer who should end the captivity of the Jews, and restore their temple and city. God had said, "of Cyrus, he is My shepherd, and shall perform all My pleasure: even saying to Jerusalem, thou shalt be built; and to the temple, thy foundation shall be laid."[3]

But how was this to be accomplished, seeing the Jews were still captives in the vast city of Babylon? The walls of Babylon were so high, it was so well defended by the

[1] B.C. 548.   [2] Herod. i. 91.   [3] Isaiah xliv. 28.

river and by its brazen gates, that it seemed impossible to enter it. The people within had provisions enough for many years.[1] But how shall men prevent what God has ordered? Cyrus had heard, that, when the bridge over the Euphrates was built at Babylon, the river had been received into a temporary lake, which had been dug some distance above the city.[2] Leaving a sufficient force, therefore, to invest the walls, he employed the rest of his army in clearing out this lake, which had now become a marsh, and in making a great cut to it from the river. When this was opened, the whole stream ran into it, and left the channel which led through the city nearly dry. Along this passage his army marched. But they still had to pass the flanking wall, which was raised within along each bank of the river, and which could only be entered, like the outer fortifications, by brazen gates. How was this difficulty to be overcome? An express prediction had long before been given; God had said, "I will loose the loins of kings, to open before him the two-leaved gates, and the gates shall not be shut."[3] The very night when Cyrus attempted to enter the city,* King Belshazzar made a great feast to a thousand of his lords, and brought forth the sacred vessels which had been taken from the temple of Jerusalem. Amidst their festivity they were off their guard; thus the girdle of their loins was loosed, and they forgot the brazen gates. The enemy entered in; Belshazzar's kingdom was taken from him, and

---

[1] Herod. i. 190.   [2] Herod. i. 191.   [3] Isaiah xlv. 1.

* The chronicle inscription recording this event is as follows:—"In the month Tammuz, Cyrus, fighting in the city of Rutu, upon the river Nizalat, to the midst of the army of Akkad he made, and fighting men on the 14th day the city of Sippara without fighting took. Nabonidus fled, and on the 16th day Gobryas, Prefect of the land of Gutium, and the soldiers of Cyrus without fighting to Babylon entered."

It was therefore the 15th day of the month Tammuz, during the night of which the entry into Babylon took place (*see* Dan. v.). This was the day of festival rejoicing for the recovery of Tammuz. It was this great heathen orgie then which Belshazzar and his lords were celebrating with the vessels and spoils from the temple of Jerusalem.

given to the Medes and Persians.[1] Thus was accomplished what God had spoken concerning Cyrus, "I will go before thee, and make the crooked places straight; I will break in pieces the gates of brass, and cut in sunder the bars of iron: and I will give thee the treasures of darkness, and hidden riches of secret places, that thou mayest know that I, the Lord, which call thee by thy name, am the God of Israel. For Jacob My servant's sake, and Israel Mine elect, I have even called thee by thy name; I have surnamed thee, though thou hast not known Me."[2]

After the taking of Babylon, the era of the complete establishment of the Persian power, Cyrus left the supreme authority nominally in the hands of Darius the Mede—according to Xenophon, his uncle, who lived, however, little more than a year longer.[3] Under both these princes Daniel was chosen to exercise the office of chief-president over the hundred and twenty princes who seem to have been appointed over the king's revenue.[4] His wisdom and incorruptness in this high office—virtues which the Persians afterwards found it scarce possible to secure in those who filled the like place—afford an example to all rulers, of the advantage of conducting public duties in the fear of God. For with all this vast burden, he found time to pray to God three times a day, and in consequence he continued "faithful, neither was there any error or fault found in him."[5] His influence may have facilitated the restoration of his nation to their own land; but the measure was so contrary to the ordinary policy of the Persians, whose object always was to break up the ties which bound together the subject-states of their empire, that its real motive can be found only in the declaration which commences the book of Ezra, that "the Lord stirred up the spirit of Cyrus, king of Persia."[6]

The seventy years, during which God had declared that

---

[1] Herod. i. 191. B.C. 538. [2] Isaiah xlv. 2-4.
[3] Dan. v. 32. [4] Dan. vi. 2. [5] Dan. vi. 4.
[6] Ezra i. 1.

Jerusalem and Judah should remain desolate, were now accomplished.[1] During many years the Jews had neglected to keep the Sabbaths which had been commanded; and when continued impunity had made them think the law forgotten, their land had been allowed this long rest during their captivity. But at length came the hour for their return, and Cyrus made proclamation that they might reoccupy their land,[2] and rebuild their temple.[3] They laid its foundation amidst the rejoicing of the young; but the old men, who remembered the first temple, wept to see how inferior was the magnificence of the new one. And yet the prophets foretold that this new house should be witness to the glory of His coming, whose presence would more than make up for the lack of earthly splendour. Daniel had been just instructed that in four hundred and thirty-four years from the completion of the temple should come that Messiah whom the temple was meant to honour.[4] "The glory of this latter house shall be greater than of the former; and in this place will I give peace, saith the Lord of Hosts."[5] The signal glory of the former house had been God's immediate presence in the holy of holies, where a cloud filled the temple. The greater glory of the second house was that our Lord appeared there in person, even as He assures us that He still does in the consecrated assemblies of His Church from age to age.

The Jews continued to build their temple during the time of Cyrus, and of Cambyses his son. The principal achievement of Cambyses was the conquest of Egypt,[6] where he put to death Psammenitus, the son of Amasis, the last prince of Egyptian blood. Amasis had rebelled against Apries[7] soon after Nebuchadnezzar's invasion of Egypt,[8] and had lately died, after a prosperous reign. With Psammenitus ended the independence of Egypt; it has

---

[1] Jeremiah; Dan. ix. 2. [2] 2 Chron. xxxvi. 21. B.C. 536.
[3] Ezra i. 2 [4] Dan. ix. 25. [5] Haggai ii. 9.
[6] B. C. 525. [7] B.C. 569. [8] *Vide* p. 51.

Persian, or Second Great Empire. 67

never since had a prince of its own, but has fulfilled Ezekiel's prophecy, that "it shall be the basest of kingdoms, neither shall it exalt itself any more above the nations."[1] "And there shall be no more a prince of the land of Egypt." But though successful in this expedition, Cambyses had made himself hated by his folly and tyranny; and on his death[2] the crown was usurped by a magian, a priest of the sun, who pretended to be Smerdis, a younger son of Cyrus. This magian, called in Scripture Artaxerxes,[3] ordered the Jews to cease from their work. But his reign was not of long continuance. His insurrection was, in truth, an attempt by covert means to restore the supreme power to the Medians, to which nation he belonged.[4] This was shortly suspected by the Persian nobles; but as he greatly resembled the son of Cyrus, whose name he had adopted, they waited for some time before taking decisive means for his destruction. In order to escape detection, he seldom left the palace. But a nobleman, whose sister he had married when he became king, desired her to feel whether he had lost his ears,[5] a punishment which had been inflicted on the magian in the time of Cyrus. She sent word that his ears had been cut off; and the chief Persians, satisfied that he was not the son of their first leader, conspired and slew him. Darius, one of the seven who had joined in this attempt, was made king by the rest.[6] They had agreed to meet on horseback, and that the one whose horse first neighed should have the crown.

This Darius, called Hystaspes, renewed the decree of Cyrus, by which the Jews were allowed to rebuild their temple.[7] He was the restorer of the Persian empire, which the magian, to gain favour with his subjects, had allowed to fall into confusion; or it may rather be said, he was the refounder of a system of which Cyrus had only left the outline:[8] for

---

[1] Ezek. xxix. 15. [2] B.C. 522. [3] Ezra iv. 21.
[4] Herod. iii. 65. [5] Herod. iii. 68. [6] B.C. 521.
[7] B.C. 519. Ezra vi. [8] Herod. iii. 67.

under Darius the Persian empire was divided into its twenty great satrapies;[1] the public revenue, which before had consisted merely of arbitrary contributions, was fixed and arranged;[2] money was coined which bore his name [Darics]; and it is probable that the roads and the public posts were then introduced,[3] by which intelligence was communicated throughout the empire. Hence the Persians, who styled Cyrus the father, and Cambyses the master, of his people, called Darius the *merchant* king.[4]

Herodotus gives a detailed account of the several nations which constituted the Persian empire,—an empire which extended south-east as far as the river Indus, northward till it touched the tribes of Scythia, and west as far as the Mediterranean Sea. Besides its tribute of money, every part of this vast country was bound to supply provisions for the king's court, his servants, and armies. The court moved according to the season of the year, spending the winter in the warmer plains of Babylon, the summer at Ecbatana in the Median mountains, the spring at Susa.[5] At each period a particular district was charged for its support, which the Babylonian province supported during four months of the year.[6] The habit of imposing on particular spots a specific duty was usual with the Persians; thus four villages were assigned to provide food for the Indian dogs of Tritanæchmes, the satrap of Babylon.[7]

The same principle which prevailed in the king's court was applied in its degree to each dependent satrap. Every one had his court; and the province was bound, besides its tribute, to give him sustenance. The satrap was possessed of almost supreme power in his own government; but as a check on his authority, the military force of the province was placed under a different officer, who was responsible only to the great king.[8] When the Persian system fell into

---

[1] Herod. iii. 89.   [2] Heeren, i. § 1. p. 417.   [3] Herod. viii. 98.
[4] Herod. iii. 89.   [5] Xenoph. Cyrop. viii. 6 § 22.
[6] Herod. i. 192.   [7] Herod. i. 192.   [8] Xenoph. Cyrop. viii. 6 § 1

confusion, these powers were sometimes united, and then the satrap became for a time an independent prince. This difficulty was experienced even in the time of Darius, at whose accession to the throne, Phrygia, Lydia, and Ionia, were in the hands of a satrap named Orœtes, who was guarded by a thousand Persians, and, though professing allegiance to the king, was acting like an independent monarch. He had put several Persians of distinction to death;[1] and a messenger sent to him with the king's orders he privately despatched. Anxious for the removal of this rebel, without the risk of a civil war, Darius stated the case to his most trusted adherents, thirty of whom immediately volunteered the destruction of Orœtes. Bagæus, who was chosen from the rest by lot for this dangerous service, provided himself with a number of various rolls, each containing an order on some subject from the king, and sanctioned by his seal.[2] With these he went to Sardis, and presented himself to Orœtes in public, when surrounded by his guards. Taking forth a roll, which related to some subject of little moment, he gave it to the royal scribe, who was always in attendance on a satrap. Perceiving that the attendant Persians displayed the greatest reverence for a document which bore the royal seal, he ventured to produce a more important order: "Persians, King Darius orders you not to act as guards to Orœtes." Seeing the attendant soldiers immediately ground their arms, Bagæus produced his last roll: "King Darius orders the Persians in Sardis to kill Orœtes,"—an injunction which the satrap's own guards instantly obeyed.

When Darius had consolidated his empire, he looked round for some means of employing the restless spirit of his subjects, and of dazzling them by the splendour of military renown.[3] With this view he marched with a large army against the Scythians, crossing into Europe by the Thracian Bosphorus (the Straits of Constantinople), and afterwards

[1] Herod. iii. 126.   [2] Herod. iii. 128.   [3] Herod. iii. 134.

passing the Danube by a bridge of boats. But the poverty of the country which he entered, inhabited only by wandering tribes, was fatal to his success; and but for the fidelity of the Ionian chiefs, whom he had left on the Danube as guards of the bridge, his whole army must have perished.[1] Herodotus marks the simplicity of manners, by relating that Darius gave the Ionians a thong containing sixty knots, bidding them to loose one a-day, and to return home when the whole number was told out. But when this was done, they learnt from a detachment of Scythians, which visited them, that Darius was involved in extreme difficulties. As the authority of the Ionian chiefs in their several cities was altogether dependent on the favour of the Persians, they were persuaded by Histiæus, the tyrant of Miletus (in opposition to the counsels of Miltiades the Athenian, who held the same office in the Thracian Chersonese), to await the king's return.

Meanwhile Darius, having advanced as far as the Volga,[2] and having afterwards pursued the Scythians into the western part of Russia, found his army perishing from fatigue and want, and that, as its strength decayed, the Scythians began to make head against him. The Scythian horsemen now attacked and discomfited the Persian cavalry, though upon infantry they were unable to make any impression. At length the Scythians sent him a herald charged with the following presents, a mouse, a bird, a frog, and five arrows. At first he hoped that this was a sign that they surrendered their earth, their air, their waters, and their military prowess. But the event soon shewed that the right interpretation was that given by Gobryas, one of the seven Persian nobles who had placed him upon the throne, "Unless you can fly like birds, or like mice can burrow under the earth, or like frogs can plunge into the waters, you will never return, but will perish by these arrows."

Alarmed by the threat, Darius followed the advice which

[1] Herod. iv. 98.   [2] Herod. iv. 124; and Rennel, p. 103.

Gobryas proceeded to give him; and leaving his sick and wounded in the night, the more active part of his army escaped to the Danube, being happily missed by the Scythians, who, reaching the river before them by a shorter course, had returned again to oppose their progress. They found the bridge still guarded by the Ionians, who had only removed it for an arrow's flight from the Scythian shore, and who, when summoned on the night of their arrival by an Egyptian, of peculiar powers of voice, in the army of Darius, soon restored it again, and provided them with the means of escape.

In the north of Europe, therefore, the poverty of the country forbade all hopes of extension for the Persian power. And from this time Darius's attention was sufficiently occupied by the Grecian tribes, in whom the Persians found that they had to do with opponents very different from those whom they had subdued in their Asiatic wars. The Greeks, who were settled on the shore of Asia Minor, had indeed been reduced either by Crœsus or Cyrus; but they now began to look for succour to the independent states on the European shore of the Ægean. Histiæus, the Milesian, who had been carried by Darius into Persia,[1] and treated there with great favour, finding that his talents and ambition exposed him to suspicion, and that he was not allowed to return home, encouraged his countrymen to revolt, in hope that to restore quiet he should be allowed to revisit them. Aristagoras, who had succeeded Histiæus, went himself to solicit assistance both at Sparta and Athens; and though at the first place he failed, yet at the second he was successful. With the aid of the Athenians, the Ionians took and burnt Sardis;[2] and though the Asiatic Greeks were afterwards conquered, yet a vast army sent by Darius, under Datis and Artaphernes, was defeated at Marathon by the Athenians.[3] They were headed by Miltiades, who had now abandoned his settle-

[1] Herod. v. 35, B.C. 499. [3] Herod. vi. 111. B.C. 490.

ment in the Thracian Chersonese, and resumed the condition of an Athenian citizen.

From this time it became apparent, that in the small and divided states of Greece there was a power which it would require all the might of the Persian empire to overcome, and the destiny of the world seemed to be dependent upon the conflict. Xerxes, therefore, who soon after succeeded his father Darius,[1] resolved to bend the whole power of his kingdom in this direction. The country was not like the Scythian desert,—a waste, where hunger was more to be dreaded than the enemy; and his great wealth enabled him to overcome all the natural obstacles which opposed his progress. For so Daniel had long before predicted. He shall "be far richer" than all that went before him, "and by his strength, through his riches, he shall stir up all against the realm of Græcia."[2] But as this is marked out by the prophet as one step in that great chain which led subsequently to the overthrow of Persia herself, and to the establishment of the third monarchy in her room, it will be necessary to state what was that hidden power which already was beginning to plume its wings for flight on the west of the Ægean, and how the empire of the world was gradually transferred from Asia to Europe.

[1] B.C. 485.   [2] Dan. xi. 2.

GRECIAN, OR THIRD GREAT EMPIRE.

GRECIAN, OR THIRD GREAT EMPIRE.

Office of the Third Empire—Character of the Greeks—Their Independence—Their Connexion—Homer—Sparta—Object and Measures of Lycurgus—Xerxes' Expedition against Greece—Numbers of his Army—Thermopylæ—Athenian Character—Solon—Pisistratus—Wooden Walls—Themistocles—Salamis—Platæa—Consequences of the Persian Expedition.

> "Immortal Greece! dear land of glorious lays,
> See here the unknown God of thy unconscious praise."
> *Christian Year.*

IN the two preceding empires there is little which, to an ordinary spectator, might seem to exercise any lasting influence on the fortunes of mankind. The history of nations seemed, indeed, to have run through two stages of more than usual importance; and twice did the wealth and power of the world find centres round which they were collected. But a new scene now presents itself. The two centuries during which the third empire was attaining its perfection gave opportunity for a grand experiment, which forms nearly the most interesting portion in the history of the world. For this was the season in which came the trial, how far the perfection of human talent, and the might of earthly law, could avail towards regenerating mankind.

The grand object of history has been stated, in these pages, to be the development of those means by which the lost image of God may be recovered. Prophecy declared, from the first, that this would be obtained through a gift to be bestowed upon one chosen people. Prophecy next took a wider range,—declared what should be the general combinations of human society—the four great forms of worldly empire,—and that they should minister in some way towards the full attainment of this heavenly blessing. The gift, indeed, was to be a gift of God, yet was human instrumentality to concur in its extension. And the first two empires had in reality done their part in this great design. The first, by early concentrating the wealth of the East, had afforded the means of setting forth the spectacle of the latter days in the middle theatre of the world. The second had acted as the preserver of that chosen people, through whom God's blessing was to be given. And now the third was to supply its portion, by providing an universal language, and by so extending the intellect of man as to enable him to do more justice to the communications of Heaven. But this it did through efforts which had another object, of which the daring design was to attain, through human means, what could only be effected through the gift of God. It is this remarkable attempt which must now be stated.

In ancient Greece mankind had attained to the greatest perfection of which mere human nature is susceptible. A climate mild, but not relaxing—a face of nature romantic, but not savage—freedom and sufficiency, such as resulted from their middle situation between the empires of the East and the barbarians of Europe,—through these circumstances it had pleased God to develop all the energies of man's nature in this portion of the seed of Japheth. They possessed an ability, and a sense of beauty, which, though it might be debased into selfishness and sensuality, yet formed also the best substratum for wisdom and purity. It was a peculiar circumstance in their history, that they were neither subject, like the nations of the East, to a single chief, nor, like the rude barbarians of the West, were destitute of national union. This independence of their several small communities resulted from those frequent migrations of their different families among one another, which prevented the establishment of any single power. At an early period of their history, the race of Agamemnon appeared likely to gain predominance; but they were afterwards ejected from their possessions by the Dorians, a different tribe of Greeks, headed by the Heraclidæ, or descendants of Hercules. These occupied the larger part of Peloponnesus, while the Ionians were masters of Attica, whence they spread to the Asiatic shore of the Ægean. Both were descended from Javan, the son of Japheth, and were those children of Elishah [Hellas] by whom "the isles of the Gentiles were divided in their lands."[1]

But along with the independence which might have issued in the loss of all community of feeling, the Grecian tribes had likewise a bond of union peculiar to themselves. This was the recollection of a common enterprise, in which, through the influence of some chiefs of the house of Pelops, their ancestors had been engaged against Troy, a city on the Asiatic shore of the Hellespont. This expedition had taken place about the time of Jephtha.[2] The Trojans were assisted by various tribes in Asia Minor; and the union of the different Grecian states against them had given a national character to the enterprise. But this feeling might have passed away, if the destruction of Troy, and the events which followed, had not been chosen by the poet Homer[3] as the subject for those great epic poems which still remain as a witness that human genius is in one respect like God's inspiration—namely, that it admits of no improvement from following times. This first of all the sublime works of man's genius still continues to be the greatest. To Homer

---

[1] B.C. 1184.   [2] Gen. x. 5.

[3] The Odyssey bears marks of a later date than the Iliad; but the difference is not greater than might have arisen within the lifetime of one man. The opinion that these poems were the works of many hands, is an instance of the ingenious arguments which may be advanced for what is manifestly false. That a single man should have been so superior as Homer to his many imitators is extraordinary; that a whole generation should have been possessed of this pre-eminence is inconceivable.

the Greeks owe the fact of their existence as a nation—he fixed their language, he embodied their national traditions, he associated them by the tie of common recollections; and to that independence which was required for the development of their energy, he united that order which was essential to their civilisation.

The national feeling, which Homer had done so much to encourage, was cherished by the ties of a common religion, by the habit of consulting the same oracle at Delphi, by the influence of a national assembly (the Amphictyons), which was connected with it, and by the public games (Olympic, Pythian, Nemean), in which all persons of Hellenic race were allowed to contend. Thus were they bound together by the tie of moral unity; as though the presiding deities of their race had selected them for the achievement of ends, and the reception of blessings, with which no foreign hands might interfere. Yet for many generations after the Trojan war, the Greeks did nothing which rendered them distinguished among the nations of the world; and that higher development of civil life, to which the independence of their several cities was conducting them, seemed for a time to exclude them from power. It excited the ridicule of Cyrus, who, comparing the want of concord which prevailed among these unconnected burghers with his own well-cemented empire, told them, when they interceded for their brethren the Asiatic Greeks, that "he had no fear of men who had a place of assembly in the midst of their city, where they met and deceived one another."[1]

Yet the Spartan state, to which Cyrus made this reply, afforded the most singular spectacle which the world had yet beheld. On the conquest of Peloponnesus by the Dorians, about eighty years after the Trojan war,[2] the country of Laconia, or Lacedæmon, had been allotted to two brothers, Euristhenes and Procles, and their followers. The descendants of these brothers ruled as joint kings;[3]

[1] Herod. i. 153.   [2] B.C. 1102.   [3] Herod. vi. 52.

but the title, in the early times of Greece, meant nothing but general in war, and first magistrate in peace, every citizen having a voice in the public determinations. The rights of a citizen, however, did not belong to every freeman who settled in the country; they were strictly hereditary, and were limited to the children of the original settlers. After the Dorian settlement, great disputes arose concerning this right in Laconia; and at length the inhabitants of Sparta obtained it as their own exclusive possession, leaving personal liberty, but without political power, to the other Lacedæmonians. (Hence they were called Periœci, *i.e.*, dwellers round about the original families.) The Helots, or inhabitants of Helos, refusing to submit, were reduced to slavery.

But the factions in Lacedæmon still continued, till Lycurgus, uncle and guardian of Charilaus, gave to the Spartans that celebrated code of laws which was the means of moulding their future character.[1] He had visited Crete, which was celebrated for its constitution, and had travelled as far as Asia Minor, to observe the manners of different states. Viewed in a political aspect, his legislation was but the application of the common principles of the Dorian race. By establishing a senate of twenty-eight elders, he gave a more aristocratical character to the constitution; but he left the principle of hereditary citizenship untouched. But it was the moral part of his system which was so remarkable. His object was to destroy those factions which had so constantly endangered the existence of the state. For this purpose it was necessary to extinguish those evil tendencies in which they originated. This could no otherwise be effected by human law, than through some system which should cut off the temptations to crime, and deprive men of those individual influences which had proved so dangerous.[2] He determined, therefore, to destroy all

---

[1] B.C. 880. Herod. i. 65.

[2] *Vide*, on this subject, Maurice's "Lectures on National Education," sect. i.

independent action; to render each man but a member of the public body; and thus to do away the incentives to crime, by destroying all the impulses of nature. He divided Laconia into thirty-nine thousand districts (nine thousand to the Spartans, and thirty thousand to the other Lacedæmonians); and by rendering them inalienable, he hoped to exclude either poverty or wealth from the families of his citizens. For the same purpose he enjoined the exclusive employment of iron money, which by its cumbrous bulk was comparatively useless. A common table; the expenditure of their time in warlike exercises; the habit of living, not as members of a private family, but as portions of a public body,—these completed Lycurgus's plan of reducing the Spartan habits to the discipline and order of a garrison in a hostile country.

But though this system prevented many crimes, it was by the sacrifice of as many virtues. For with the worst, the Spartans lost the best part of humanity. The arts of life, the desire of knowledge, the ties of domestic love, the affections which purify and ennoble the mind, were destroyed. Yet in one respect the purpose of Lycurgus was answered. Sparta became a powerful city; its inhabitants were free from the disturbances which weakened the rest of Greece; so that, by the time of the Persian expedition, the universal consent of its other states conceded to them the pre-eminence.[1] But for them and the Athenians, the Persian power would not have been resisted. When Darius first aimed at the subjection of the Greeks, he sent heralds to demand earth and water, as a sign of submission:[2] at Athens and Sparta they were roughly treated; but the islanders, and a considerable portion of the continental Greeks, gave this token of obedience. And now the Spartans prepared to oppose the countless host with which Xerxes threatened Greece; and as a public festival prevented them from marching immediately against him, they sent

[1] Herod, vii. 159, and viii. 2. [2] Herod. vi. 49, and vii. 133.

Grecian, or Third Great Empire.

Leonidas, one of their kings, with three hundred Spartans, and a small force of their allies, to occupy the pass of Thermopylæ.[1]

Meanwhile Xerxes led on his vast army,[2] in the preparation of which the whole East had been engaged during several years.[3] Having passed the winter at Sardis, he prepared in the spring to cross the Hellespont by a bridge of boats formed by his Phœnician and Egyptian fleets, opposite to Abydos.[4] But just as he was about to pass, his bridge was broken, and the vessels which composed it dispersed by a storm. Xerxes, in an access of passion, beheaded those who had superintended its preparation; and, whether from pride or childish petulance, ordered chains to be cast, and scourges inflicted, upon the Hellespont. His army crossed the bridge so soon as it was renewed, consuming in the passage seven days and nights. The plains of Doriscus in Thrace, on the banks of the Hebrus, afforded him a place for mustering its numbers. Ten thousand men were collected in one spot, round which a fence was drawn, and then the same space was re-occupied by another body, till the whole had passed. The whole number of fighting-men was about two millions and a half, and at least as numerous were the attendants. Never was host composed of materials so various: "Ethiopians from the south of Egypt in the skins of lions, and Indians in their cotton garments; their dark neighbours from Gedrosia, mixed with the wandering Scythians from Bucharia; the wild Sagartian hunters, who, without weapons either of stone or iron, entangled their enemies in leathern thongs, like the harts which they hunted; Medes and Bactrians in their rich garments; Libyans in their four-horse cars; and Arabians on their camels."[5] To this must be added, a fleet of twelve hundred and seven ships, drawn from

[1] Herod. vii. 201.
[2] B.C. 481.
[3] Herod. vii. 1 and following chapters.
[4] B.C 480.
[5] Heeren, "Ideen," i. § i. 5 8.

the tributary Greeks, and from the ports of Egypt and Phœnicia.

Against such an armament as this Xerxes supposed that the Greeks would not attempt opposition. When he reached Thermopylæ, and found Leonidas at the head of a body of about four thousand men from Peloponnesus, he waited four days, expecting that they would fly at his approach. The majority, indeed, were disposed to retreat; but Leonidas determined to remain, for the protection of the neighbouring region of Locris. At the same time, the Grecian fleet was stationed in the narrow passage between Eubœa and the continent. When Xerxes found that his way was opposed by this small body of Greeks, he ordered his Median and Cissian soldiers to take them and bring them before him alive. And now, for the first time, he learnt the effects of that resolution and discipline which the Spartans had acquired from the institutions of Lycurgus. When, in the closing contest, his best troops were again and again defeated by this handful of men, his agitation became so great, that he sprung up in alarm from the seat which he occupied within view of the battle, fearing that the flower of his army would perish from their wondrous prowess. "How many of these Lacedæmonians remain?" he said afterwards to Demaratus, who, having been king of Sparta and deprived of the throne, was now a fugitive in his court:[1] "are the whole nation of the same valour with those who have fallen?" "The whole body of the Lacedæmonians," replied Demaratus, "is considerable, and their cities numerous. But the capital of Lacedæmon is Sparta a city containing about eight thousand persons. All of these are exactly like those who have fought here." This was a true answer; for the resolution of these three hundred warriors was but a part of that public heroism which lived in every Spartan breast. Of this they gave proof, when the Persians had at length surrounded them, by sending a de-

[1] Herod. vii. 234.

tachment over a pass among the mountains. Leonidas sent back his allies, except seven hundred Thespians, who refused to leave him; but he himself determined to remain with his small body of men, that he might give a lasting evidence of the unconquerable firmness of the Spartan discipline. After an immense slaughter of the enemy, he and his three hundred Spartans were slain to a man; and the following epitaph, erected on the spot by the general council of the Greek nation, subsequently recorded their motive:

> "Stranger, our hest to Sparta bear, and tell
> That here obedient to her laws we fell."

After passing Thermopylæ, Xerxes directed his march against Attica; one principal object of his expedition being to revenge himself on the Athenians, who had taken part with the Ionians in the destruction of Sardis, and had since defeated the Persians at Marathon. Had the Athenians yielded to his arms, as from their exposed situation might have been expected, and thus given into his hands their ships, which constituted the larger part of the Grecian fleet, the valour of the Peloponnesians would not, in the opinion of Herodotus,[1] have been of any avail. On Athens, he says, depended the safety of Greece. And the determination of Athens depended, in great measure, on one leading mind, which was providentially raised up for this national emergency. For the Athenians, being free from every outward restraint, were, like other great bodies of men, the prey of any one who possessed the peculiar talent of persuading them that what he suggested was their own individual will. It was impossible to conceive a greater contrast than they afforded to the Lacedæmonians. In Sparta every thing was for strength, and greater resolution human nature could not conceive; in Athens all was freedom, and a resistless elasticity of the individual mind. Athens, too, had in Solon[2] possessed a lawgiver of consummate wisdom;

[1] Herod. vii. 139. [2] Died B.C. 559.

but he had found it impossible to bridle that which was the predominant characteristic of Athenian nature, the full development of private will. His legislation had been more artificial than any which had preceded it, and resulted from the observations of a man of great ability on the institutions of foreign countries,[1] as well as on the complicated relations of Grecian politics. While giving to all citizens a voice in the government, he had endeavoured to curb their excesses, by requiring that public officers should be chosen out of the wealthier of those classes into which he had divided them; by the appointment of a senate; and still more by the restraining and censorial power of the court of Areopagus. But his institutions were almost immediately impaired by the seditions raised by Pisistratus,[2] who, gaining over the lower orders, set himself above the law, and became tyrant of Athens. This title his children continued to bear for fifty years; though at times driven from their post by the powerful family of Alcmæon, whose leader Clisthenes in his turn courted the people by further alterations in Solon's constitution. At length, twenty-four years before the battle of Marathon,[3] Hipparchus, one of the sons of Pisistratus, was murdered by Harmodius and Aristogiton; and Hippias, the other son, was soon afterwards driven from the city.[4] And now the Athenians entered upon the enjoyment of complete liberty. They were able to give the fullest and most favourable specimen of the effect of republican institutions, just as Sparta did of the tendencies of a military aristocracy; because in both cases the attendance of a vast body of slaves gave to the freemen a leisure and independence, which enabled them to devote their undivided attention to public events. A census of the inhabitants of Athens, taken at a later period,[5] gives but twenty-one thousand

---

[1] He borrowed from Egypt the plan of a "census," which afterwards passed to Rome. Herod. ii. 177.
[2] B.C. 560.   [3] B.C. 514.   [4] B.C. 510.   [5] Mitford, v. 4.

citizens, while the slaves are stated to be four hundred thousand.[1]

In Athens, therefore, as before in Sparta, we see exhibited whatever was striking in the Grecian character. Exquisite taste, unequalled talent, eloquence such as the world has not elsewhere witnessed, profound speculation, daring enterprise, heroic courage,—all these were combined with every thing which can disgust and affright the mind. And as there never was a state where men were better trained than in Sparta to serve the public, so never were there men who lived more than the Athenians to delight themselves. Yet as in Sparta it was a generous service, rendered by freemen to their native land, so the Athenians were too noble a people to be satisfied with mere sensual delight. The arts and sciences, the cultivation of the understanding, and the honours of military renown, were among their choicest gratifications. The Greek language, as uttered by them, was the most majestic employment of man's common gift of speech since the creation of the world; and so refined was their perception of its beauty, that the distinguished orator Theophrastus, after spending the larger part of his life at Athens, found, to his mortification, that a simple market-woman could detect in an instant that his ear had not been accustomed in youth to the dialect of Attica.[2] A people so free from outward restraint might have been expected to shrink from the hardships and losses with which the Athenians were now threatened. But their conduct exhibits an instance of the sacrifices which a high-minded people will consent to make, when they feel themselves directed by a man of commanding genius. Such a man was Themistocles, who having long formed the design of rendering his countrymen a great naval power, and having induced them some years before to apply their revenue to

---

[1] Reckoning heads of families only to be counted as citizens, this would make the slaves about four times their number.

[2] Cicero, Brutus, iv. § 6.

the formation of a navy,[1] now persuaded them to embark whatever they could carry with them, and trusting themselves to their "wooden walls," to abandon Attica to the conqueror.[2] They joined the rest of the Grecian fleet at Salamis; but Themistocles found it difficult to retain the favourable position which the narrow passage between this island and the mainland afforded to the Grecian fleet in its contest with the more numerous armament of Xerxes. The other Grecians, alarmed by the vast force which was approaching, wished to fly to the Isthmus of Corinth, which the Peloponnesians were preparing to fortify, and would thus have fought at great disadvantage in an open sea. Themistocles, in consequence, sent private information of their intended flight to Xerxes; and thus, under pretence of enabling the Persians to surround them in the strait which divided Salamis from the continent, compelled his countrymen to an immediate conflict. On the Persian side were many Grecian vessels from its subject-states in Ionia, but its great force was from Phœnicia and the neighbouring shores of the Mediterranean. The Phœnicians had now an opportunity of gratifying their ill-will against the Greeks, to whom they had been compelled to yield their earliest seats of traffic, and whom, whenever opportunity offered, they ever pursued with rancorous hatred.[3] But their hostility and superior numbers did but afford a clearer proof of the ascendency of the Grecian character. They were the first to fly before the onset of the Athenians, and involved the total defeat of the Persian fleet.

With the ruin of his fleet Xerxes in great measure abandoned his hopes of success. Leaving Mardonius with an army of three hundred thousand Asiatics and fifty thousand tributary Greeks, he himself returned to Sardis. And now came the time for the final display of Grecian courage.[4] Under the guidance of the Lacedæmonians, headed by

---

[1] Herod. vii. 144.
[2] Herod. vii. 143; viii. 41.
[3] Herod. v. 42, 46.
[4] B.C. 479.

Pausanias, the guardian of their young king, an army was collected of about forty thousand heavy-armed and seventy thousand light-armed troops. By this army Mardonius was totally defeated and slain near Platæa in Bœotia; the native Persians in his army fighting with great valour, but having neither armour nor discipline to contend with the well-trained force of the Spartans. The Persians once broken, the other Asiatics made no attempt at resistance:

> " The daring Greeks deride the martial show,
> And heap their valleys with the insulting foe."

And while the larger part of the army of Xerxes was thus destroyed in Bœotia, the Grecian fleet had already passed the Ægean, where the Persians, who had returned, or who had been collected on the shore of Asia Minor, were defeated on the very same day, in a great battle at Mycale.

The attempt, therefore, of Asia to subject Greece ended only in the assertion of its independence and superiority. Like the Trojan war, this Persian conflict bound together its different tribes, and gave them yet higher grounds for glorying in their common country. Henceforth they felt that some great destiny lay before it. At the commencement of the struggle, the unknown power of the great king was viewed with such apprehension that no people had dared to withstand the assault of the conquerors of Asia, till the Athenians set the example in the plains of Marathon.[1] But now it was no longer doubtful that the ascendency rested with the natives of the West. It remained only to determine what tribe should lead forth the sons of Europe, and what state should be the head of that empire which should arise out of Greece for the subjugation of mankind.

[1] Herod. vi. 112.

ATHENIAN ATTEMPT AT ESTABLISHING THE GRECIAN EMPIRE.

Spartans unfit for Rule—Aristides—Athens Fortified—Allies rendered Dependent—Athenian and Spartan Alliance—Peloponnesian War—Brasidas—Alcibiades—Sicilian Expedition—Ægospotamos—Athens taken.

> " On the Ægean shore a city stands—
> Athens, the eye of Greece, mother of arts
> And eloquence, native to famous wits
> Or hospitable, in her sweet recess
> City or suburban, studious walks and shades."—MILTON.

THE retreat of Xerxes left the rule of Greece in the hands of the Spartans; and their general, Pausanias, headed the expedition which proceeded to free the cities of the Hellespont and of Asia Minor. After delivering Cyprus he proceeded to the siege of Byzantium.[1] But here his conduct shewed the inevitable weakness of the institutions of Lycurgus, and that it is little to remove the occasion, without removing the disposition, to offend. On the taking of Byzantium, some Persian captives of distinction gained over Pausanias by the hopes of wealth and luxury, such as he never could enjoy as a Spartan citizen; and he soon offended the other Greeks, by what in subsequent times was their common complaint, that, "strict as was the Spartan discipline at home, its citizens were no sooner sent to command in foreign countries, than they forgot not only their own severer rules, but even those common principles of duty which were regarded by the other Greeks."

In Aristides the Athenian, who had held an inferior command under Pausanias, the allies had the example of a man as superior to his countrymen as the Spartan general fell below them. To him, therefore, and to Athens they now

[1] B.C. 470. Thucydides, i. 94.

came, and committed to them the authority, which before they would yield to none but a Lacedæmonian.[1] So that Aristides gained for himself the title of the just; and "for his country, what it never before possessed, the dominion of the sea."[2] Nor had Themistocles been of less national advantage to his citizens. When they returned to Attica, on the retreat of Xerxes, the Lacedæmonians wished to prevent the fortification of their city, professedly lest fortified places out of Peloponnesus should hereafter afford harbour to the Persians, but in reality out of jealousy of their rising power. It was by the artful delays of Themistocles, who himself went as ambassador to Sparta, that the Lacedæmonians were prevented from enforcing their demand till the Athenians had raised their walls to a defensible height. The completion of their fortifications was followed by the improvement of their harbours, which were joined to the city by lofty walls; and thus Athens gained almost the security of an insular power.

The subsequent advance of its greatness, during the forty-five years which elapsed from the commencement of its command till the Peloponnesian war, was the work of those great men who successively rose up for its direction. But if the extraordinary elasticity of the Athenian constitution led to the existence of great men, the fickleness and ingratitude of the people prevented them from profiting as they might by their abilities. Miltiades, the victor of Marathon, died in prison. Aristides the just had been banished before the Persian war. The same fate befell Themistocles, the saviour of his country, soon after it. Cimon, son of Miltiades, who took the greatest lead in the formation of the Athenian empire, suffered for considerable time under a similar sentence. He had commanded in various expeditions which had established the authority of the Athenians over the various allies which made up their confederacy. They had begun by establishing a common

---

[1] Thucydides, i. 95, *et sq.* Herod. viii. 3.   [2] Diod. xi. 6.

treasury at Delos, and assigning to each state a contribution of ships or money, with a view to defence against the Persians. But they soon transferred the treasury to their own city; they extended the money-payment, with a view of increasing their own navy, and they inflicted the severest punishment on any states which withheld it. Naxos and Thasos, the first to revolt, were made an example to others.

Meanwhile the energy of the people was increased by the change which had taken place in their domestic institutions. The dissolution of ancient ties and hereditary associations, produced by their confinement on shipboard, and by the destruction of their city, had given an impulse to the democratical party, which led to the removal of that qualification which Solon had made essential to office. The authority of the court of Areopagus, which he had established as a check upon the democracy, was greatly diminished. At the same time the popular mind was swayed by Pericles, a statesman who, though not superior to the temptation of being the public favourite, was yet thoroughly free from every mercenary motive, and desirous only of advancing the splendour and strength of Athens. So rapidly was this effected that at the commencement of the Peloponnesian war, the Athenian alliance embraced Chios, Samos, Lesbos, all the islands of the Archipelago (except Thera and Melos, which took no part), Corcyra, Zacynthus, the Greek colonies in Asia Minor and on the coasts of Thrace and Macedonia, and in Greece itself, Acarnania, and the cities of Naupactus and Plataea. Besides these, which with few exceptions were subject states, they had a party in many cities of the Lacedæmonian alliance—the democratical faction everywhere looking up to Athens as its only hope of predominance.

This feeling, however, was kept in check by that national jealousy with which all the tribes of Dorian blood looked upon their Ionian origin. This tie, and the love of

Athenian Attempt at Establishing Grecian Empire. 91

aristocratical institutions, formed the connecting bond of the Spartan alliance. It included all Peloponnesus except Achaia and Argos, which stood neuter—Megara, Locris, Phocis, Bœotia, the towns of Ambracia and Anactorium, and the island of Leucadia. These powerful confederacies had long looked on one another with suspicion before they finally encountered in the Peloponnesian war. The wisest leaders on each side desired to prevent hostilities. Pericles perceived that the great danger of Athens arose from its inordinate ambition, and that its wisest policy was slowly to cement its empire, by gaining more complete command over its subject states. On the other hand, the Spartan king Archidamus pointed out to his countrymen that they had no means of aggression except to ravage the lands of Attica, of which the Athenians, commanding the sea, were independent, while they would be exposed to every species of injury without power of retaliation.

But the violence of both parties soon led them into a war which lasted twenty-seven years, and verified the predictions of both leaders.[1] The Peloponnesians ravaged Attica; but as the Athenians were not allowed by Pericles, then their general, to leave the walls and oppose them, no further injury could be inflicted. Meanwhile the Athenian ships ravaged every part of the Lacedæmonian coast. Nor did any means offer for injuring the Athenians till there arose a Spartan, who, to the firmness and self-possession which belonged to his countrymen, displayed a pliability of mind, an enterprise, and a readiness to avail himself of every resource, for which he was not indebted to the discipline of Lycurgus.[2] Brasidas, such was his name, was sent with a small force into Thrace; and after making his way through the hostile plains of Thessaly, he succeeded in alienating many of its towns from Athens. He had gained possession of Amphipolis, a port of great importance on the river Strymon, commanding the sole

[1] B.C. 431.   [2] Thucyd. iv. 65 and following. B.C. 424.

passage along the Thracian shore, when Cleon, an Athenian demagogue, who, after the death of Pericles, had gained great influence with the populace, was sent against him. Cleon, a tanner by trade, wholly ignorant of military measures, exposed his forces to certain defeat by defiling in front of Amphipolis, so as to lay open their right or unguarded sides to the arrows of the enemy. Brasidas sallied forth to take advantage of the error, and exposing himself in the hurry of the attack, he fell,—a loss as irreparable to the Spartans as the death of Cleon was beneficial to their enemies.

But at this time there arose a man better fitted to represent the peculiar combination of talent and volatility which belonged to the Athenian character. Alcibiades, son of Clinias, was an Athenian of birth and fortune, who possessed the still more important qualifications of courage, talent, and eloquence. He quickly became a favourite with the multitude; and after various negotiations in Peloponnesus, which proved his great ascendency over the minds of men, he engaged his countrymen in an expedition against the island of Sicily,[1] which, if he had been allowed to carry his designs into execution, would probably have confirmed them in the empire of Greece; but which their suspicion and inconstancy made the means of their destruction.[2] Pericles had advised them not to risk their forces on any great attempt till the conclusion of the Peloponnesian war. Alcibiades had extensive plans for making the conquest of Sicily a means for that of Peloponnesus. But the Athenians would neither regard the prudent caution of the one, nor give scope to the daring designs of the other. They sent the greater part of their forces to Sicily. But they soon recalled Alcibiades, whose talents alone sufficed for their direction. The Syracusans, a colony of Dorian extraction, encouraged, when on the eve of ruin, by the presence of Gylippus, a Lacedæmonian,

[1] B.C. 415. Thucyd. vi. &c. [2] Thucyd. ii. 65.

made head successfully against them, and the expedition ended in the total destruction of their fleet and army.[1] Meanwhile Alcibiades, returning to Greece, and flying as an exile to Sparta, imparted Athenian energy to its drooping counsels. Still, though they were deserted by many of their allies, their cause might have prevailed, had not their inconstancy disgusted their best generals, and again alienated Alcibiades, whom the prevalence of the aristocratical party had recalled to Athens. At length the strength of Sparta, aided by Persian gold, enabled Lysander to collect an armament, by which their last fleet was defeated at Ægospotamos in the Hellespont, and they were finally blockaded by sea and land.[2] After a protracted siege, in which they suffered all the miseries of famine, while they anticipated the retribution of those cruelties which they had inflicted on other Grecian states (as Melos, a Lacedæmonian colony, where they had put all the male citizens to death),—the Athenians were finally compelled to surrender their city. But the recollection of their services in the Persian war was not totally effaced. The Spartans declared that they would not put out one of the eyes of Greece. They contented themselves with the demolition of the long walls, which had secured Athens from their power, and with imposing such other conditions as established their own supremacy in Greece.

[1] B.C. 413.   [2] B.C. 403. Xenophon's "Hellenics," i. and ii.

THE SPIRITUAL KINGDOM OF THE GRECIAN PHILOSOPHERS.

Attempt to Improve Man's Character—Poetry and the Arts—Their little effect—Plague at Athens—The Sophists—Pythagoras—Ionic School—Socrates—The Four Schools of his Disciples—Plato—Philosophy fails of raising Human Nature.

"Be assured that those things, which by his treacherous artifices he who is called the Tempter has caused to be uttered among the Greeks, have only added to my knowledge and belief in the Scriptures."—JUSTIN MARTYR's *Dialogue with Trypho*, 69.

THE daring attempt of the Athenians to concentrate in their city the power of the west had thus signally failed. Democracy had given them confidence and energy for the attempt, but wanted prudence and self-restraint for its execution. The oath required of their youth, "to regard wheat, barley, vines, and olives as the only boundaries of Attica," as though "all the cultivated parts of the world"[1] must submit to their sway, became henceforth an idle boast.

But in the meantime there had arisen, in the heart of this adventurous republic, a set of men who proposed to themselves a different sort of empire over mankind, and who, in truth, bore a great part in that mighty alteration which the third empire was to produce on the fortunes of the world. Both by what they did, and by what they failed of effecting, the Greek philosophers carried on the designs of God's providence; they diffused that universal language which opened a way for the triumphs of the Gospel, and they shewed that nothing but the Gospel could enlighten mankind.

The minds of the Greeks had first been cultivated by poetry and the arts. Pisistratus made it his object to render

---

[1] Gillies' "Greece," chap. xiii.

the poems of Homer popular at Athens, as the same method had been taken by Lycurgus to improve the Lacedæmonians. But the military system of Sparta had suited little with the elegant arts, which had taken full root at Athens. There Pericles taught the people to expend their public resources on adorning their city. There was this peculiar excellence in ancient times, that works of art were not made subservient, as among the moderns, to the selfishness of private luxury, but were either employed to give greater dignity to public law or greater sanctity to religious worship. At this time, accordingly, the Parthenon, the pride of ancient architecture, was built in honour of their tutelary goddess Minerva; and Phidias, the greatest sculptor of antiquity, honoured Athens at this period by his abode and his works. Its great dramatic poets, Æschylus, Sophocles, and Euripides, and Aristophanes, the author of the most celebrated comedies, flourished or arose during the age of Pericles. The war with Sparta was narrated by their citizen Thucydides, the chief of Greek historians. But these, and a host besides them, of distinguished men, did little to raise the moral character of the people. Their ingratitude to their principal leaders has been described. And a pestilence, which assailed Athens at the commencement of the Peloponnesian war, shewed that, in what constitutes man's character for good or evil, they were inferior to many of the most unenlightened barbarians.

Thucydides, himself resident in Athens at the time of the plague,[1] describes its progress and consequences. Many countries were visited by it; but the Athenians, driven within the narrow circuit of their walls by the Lacedæmonian forces, experienced peculiar sufferings. After mentioning the neglect, and the interference with the ordinary rites of burial, which resulted from its ravages, Thucydides observes, "that this pestilence in other particulars also opened the door for great corruption in the city; for each one ventured

[1] B.B. 431-429.

with more readiness on the indulgence of those desires which he had formerly concealed, seeing such sudden transitions—men being one day rich and the next departed, while those who had before been in poverty entered upon their possessions. They thought, therefore, that what could be immediately enjoyed, and what gave pleasure, was the only thing worth pursuing, since their lives and their estates were but the possessions of a day. No one felt any zeal to labour for the sake of honour, since it was so uncertain whether his life would suffice for the attainment of his end; but instant gratification, and whatever afforded the means of its attainment, came to be thought both honourable and useful. The fear of the gods and the laws of men ceased alike to be restraints: the former, because it seemed indifferent whether it was entertained or not, since the pious and the impious were seen equally to perish; the latter, because no one expected to live long enough to suffer retribution for his offences, seeing that a much greater sentence was already impending, and that it was natural to obtain such enjoyment as he could of life before its penalty was inflicted."[1]

Such was the condition of the polished Athenians, among whom the beams of natural conscience had been almost obscured, while no better light had been given for their guidance. Their character had been greatly injured by the Sophists, persons who for hire taught eloquence and the arts of argument, with a perfect indifference whether they were used for the furtherance of truth or the propagation of falsehood. These men had managed to be received as the proper instructors of youth; and the rising generation at Athens, instead of being trained in the simple rural habits of a former age, had in consequence become arrogant, without possessing more real knowledge, and better talkers than their parents, with less of purity, affection, and truth. The name of Sophists was derived from that of *sophoi*, or wise

[1] Thucyd. ii. 53.

men, which had been given a century before to the first Greeks who had cultivated moral and political science. These wise men, of whom Thales and Solon were the most distinguished, had directed their main attention to the state of civil society; and certain maxims, in which they expressed the result of their moral reflections, are recorded as among the first of prose compositions. But besides these practical inquiries, they taught their countrymen to think; and out of the legends of the poets, mixed with the observations of life, various theories were formed respecting the origin of external objects. Hence there arose two main schools—the Ionian, in the country where most of the "wise men" had dwelt; and the Italian, of which Pythagoras, the first who took the name of philosopher (lover of wisdom), was the great ornament. He had lived long in Egypt, and studied its learning; and it seems probable that, either directly or indirectly, he obtained a measure of knowledge from the Jewish Scriptures. He taught what is called the doctrine of metempsychosis, that the soul of man did not perish, but that it passed into other bodies. Removing to Crotona in Italy when in his prime of life, he founded a society which aimed at effecting, by a new course, what the institute of Lycurgus had failed to perform. Believing with Aristotle,[1] that the multitude could never be directed but by compulsion, he associated to himself about three hundred of the principal citizens of Crotona and the neighbouring states, and attempted to mould them into a superior society, which should be governed by higher motives. His measures effected a great improvement in that part of Italy where he was settled: and his principle of abandoning the great mass of the people, and aiming at the benefit of men of superior natures, promised to produce wide effects. But public jealousy was awakened by his designs; some who were excluded from his narrow circle excited the many against

[1] Nicomachæan Ethics, x. 9.

him; and his system was overthrown, and his followers persecuted, by the populace.

The Ionian school did not produce similar effects; but it had its succession of sages, of whom Anaxagoras, the master of Pericles, was the chief. He taught in Athens during its greatest splendour, and was the first to maintain the unity of the Supreme Being—a doctrine which the corruptions of the popular polytheism had concealed. Of the same school was Archelaus, among whose disciples was Socrates, a man who was raised up to perform whatever could be performed by human efforts against those Sophists by whom his countrymen were deluded. Socrates was the greatest man whom mere human nature has ever produced —a man as distinguished for his private purity, his humility and affection, as for the largeness of his views, his command over his fellow-creatures, his vigour and courage. Unlike most other teachers, he wrote nothing. He left no sect to bear his name. He was not anxious, like the Sophists, to be himself distinguished for learning or eloquence, but that all whom he knew should seek truth and love it. He felt himself charged with a mission, he knew not whence, for this great object. Hence he was the founder of the school of reflective men. Instead of vain questions respecting the origin of things, on which the philosophers of the Ionian and Italian schools had been principally occupied, he taught his disciples to look into their inward being, and to discern in mankind the reality of a moral nature. His followers describe him as instructing men to pray for guidance to some unrevealed power,[1]—that "unknown God," whom St. Paul afterwards preached in the selfsame city,— and as expecting some further intimations of its will. He taught the certainty of a future state,[2] and the necessity of preparing for it. Thus was he visited by that light which was afterwards in full perfection to come into the world, but of which we read, that from the beginning it was the "light

[1] Plato, second Alcibiades. [2] Plato, Phædo.

of men." Hence was he the apostle of conscience. From this source did he derive that "sage philosophy," of which Milton declares, that it

> "From heaven descended to the low-roofed hut
>   Of Socrates: see there his tenement,
>   Whom well-inspired the oracle pronounced
>   Wisest of men; from whose mouth issued forth
>   Mellifluous streams, that watered all the schools
>   Of Academics old and new, with those
>   Surnamed Peripatetic, and the sect
>   Epicurean, and the Stoic severe."

The Academics were a sect of Philosophers who followed the teaching of Socrates's favourite disciple, Plato. He wrote a book called the "Polity," in which he mixed some things drawn from Jewish sources with the teaching of his master. His object was to set forth a perfect exhibition of what *might* be man's estate,—a pattern and model of the moral world. All notions of excellence which had been exhibited by Spartan rigour or Athenian liberty were here moulded together by consummate genius and the deepest reflection of a meditative mind. Xenophon's Cyropædia (education of Cyrus) is an attempt to embody the same great idea in the history of the origin and plan of the Persian state. So that as Greece had before displayed what laws could effect, it now taught what philosophy could perform. The plan of educating men to do their duty, to love truth, to serve nature, to reverence God's law written in their conscience, to detect and follow the lingering traces of aboriginal purity and happiness,—all this is set forth with a fulness and eloquence which still continues to be the admiration of mankind. So that nothing could by natural means be added to what the philosophers and legislators of Greece had devised for the regeneration of man.

"Vain wisdom all, and false philosophy."

It was a fair statue, but it wanted life. An universe was designed in all the perfection of form, but there was no sun to quicken it into warmth and beauty. The system of the ancients continues, indeed, to be of unequalled use in the education of Christians; because while it shews what unaided man could effect, and calls forth the imitative energies of the noblest natures, it sheds thereby a clearer light on those truths which man cannot attain, and proves them to be the exclusive consequence of divine illumination. But of itself, it was utterly inefficacious for restoring God's image in His degenerate creatures. It was without moving power. It was only the "sounding brass," which Daniel had made the symbol of the third empire. Alas for the folly of those who, when the Sun of righteousness has arisen, would still devise a "moral world," without taking advantage of His beams! Greater men than they have tried it without success. But the blinded Socialist goes forth at noonday, and thinks that his glimmering rushlight illuminates the world; whereas when night really prevailed, not even the burning genius of a Socrates or Plato could disperse the darkness. What but the pure light of that Christian faith against which he shuts his eyes preserves him from those public and signal evils, of which the most enlightened age of Greece, and its wisest teachers, were the victims. The genius of the Athenians did not save them from the disgrace of destroying Socrates, the wisest and best of their citizens.[1] To him, who did not regard death as a loss, but rather life as a duty, this was no evil; but it taught how little man's reason had effected for the recovery of the world.

The same lesson was taught by the subsequent course of philosophy. Four chief schools of opinion arose: that of Plato; the Peripatetic, formed by his disciple Aristotle; the Stoic; and Epicurean. The first two of these took the purer and better view of things: Plato looking at human nature rather on the side of those natural feelings of right and wrong, which are the chief remains of God's image in

[1] B.C. 400.

the mind; and Aristotle trusting chiefly to men's powers of reasoning, and to such truths as could be deduced from argument. But the Stoics and Epicureans had more influence upon life. The Stoic rule was a sort of application of the Spartan system to the inward nature—its ground man's pride and self-sufficiency; while the Epicureans undertook the defence of man's sensual tendencies, and provided a justification for every vice. Against these two last sects, therefore, the arguments of the apostle of the Gentiles were specially directed: "Certain philosophers of the Epicureans and of the Stoics encountered him."[1] And while many followers of Plato entered the early Church, it drew few recruits from the proud or sensual schools of philosophy. Yet did these spread abroad, and fill Athens and Greece with their doctrine. So that, notwithstanding the light bestowed upon them in Socrates, this ingenious people became less moral and more besotted than the rest of the nations. Public spirit faded away among them. The experiment of raising man's nature had been tried, and tried without success. And thus ended the vain attempt to attain through philosophy those great results which the kingdom of Christ could alone supply.

[1] Acts xvii. 18.

[Hardly enough weight seems to be attached in this *resumé* of ancient systems of philosophy to the consideration of their place in the history of the thought of the world as preparations for the truth of the Incarnation. It is remarkable at least that the Platonists' doctrine of the word should have so nearly approached to Christian Revelation (see "Confessions of St. Augustine," book vii., chap. 9); and their teachings on the subject of conscience and providence did effect something in the way of a prepared soil, in which the seed of Christian Truth might later germinate and bear fruit. The Hebrew Prophet, through special inspiration, gave forth declarations of "Him that should come:" the Greek philosopher, "feeling after Him, if haply he might find Him," fulfilled an analogous office in respect to those whom he taught, and whom the Prophets of an alien, and, as it seemed, uncultured race, could never have reached. It is evident from the manner of St. Paul on Mars' Hill, that he recognised in the teaching of the philosophers something, which, though in itself insufficient, might be made of service

RETREAT OF THE TEN THOUSAND—THEBES AIMS AT THE EMPIRE OF GREECE.

State of Persia—Ezra—Old Testament completed—Cyrus the Younger—Battle of Cunaxa—Persian Treachery—Xenophon—Return of Greeks—Agesilaus—Thebes—Epaminondas—Improvement in the Art of War—Leuctra—Laconia Ravaged—Mantinæa.

"During the reign of Cleomenes, Sparta was visited by Aristagoras, the tyrant of Miletus, who had with him, as the Lacedæmonians say, a brazen tablet, on which was engraved an outline of the whole circumference of the earth, the whole sea, and all rivers. Admitted to an interview with the king, Aristagoras said to him, 'Cleomenes, marvel not at the anxiety which has brought me here. The case is this: that the Ionians should be slaves instead of freemen, is the greatest disgrace and grief to ourselves, and next to you, since you are the leaders of Greece. I beseech you, then, by the Grecian gods, to deliver your kinsmen, the Ionians, from slavery. The task is one which you may easily perform; for the Barbarians are not warlike, while you have the highest reputation for valour.' [He then shewed, in his map, the countries which intervene between the Egean sea and Susa.] When the time came for giving an answer, Cleomenes asked Aristagoras how many days' journey it was from the Ionian sea to the king's dwelling. Aristagoras, subtle as he was in the rest of the conference, and skilful in his artifices, was caught by this question. If he wished to draw the Spartans into Asia, he ought not to have betrayed the real state of the case; whereas he declared it plainly, saying, 'that the journey up would require three months.' Cleomenes, cutting short what he was going to add, replied, 'Milesian stranger, depart from Sparta before sunset: for it is no acceptable proposal which you make to the Lacedæmonians, when you wish to lead them three months' journey from the sea.'"— HEROD. v. 49, 50.

WHILE the Greeks were ineffectually contending for the possession of anticipated empire, the Persian power was gradually losing the vigour of youth, without

to the truth; and so displayed his faith in St. John's declaration, that "He is the true Light which lighteth every man that cometh into the world."]

acquiring the wisdom of age. Its great work—the restoration of God's chosen people—had long been completed. Artaxerxes, the son of Xerxes, called Ahasuerus in the narrative of his marriage with Queen Esther,[1] had sent Ezra the scribe to Jerusalem,[2] and afterwards appointed Nehemiah as its governor; and by their means was the temple and city finally restored. In their days,[3] too, a still greater work was accomplished: the volume of the Old Testament was completed; the prophecies of Zechariah and Malachi were added to what had been given before; and thus was the first part of God's revelation sealed up, to wait for its enlargement in the latter days.

The succession of the Persian princes was often interrupted—as was usual in the absolute dynasties of Asia—by intrigue and assassination; and by such means, Darius Ochus, an illegitimate son of Artaxerxes, succeeded in gaining his father's throne after the death of two of his brothers.[4] This prince, who reigned during the Peloponnesian war, committed the satrapy of Lydia and the seacoast of Ionia to Cyrus, his younger son. Cyrus it was who had assisted the Lacedæmonians with money towards the end of the Peloponnesian war; and he hoped, by invoking the aid of Grecian valour, to succeed his father on the throne of Persia. Darius died about the time of the taking of Athens;[5] and Cyrus solicited and obtained some aid in his designs from the Lacedæmonians.[6] But his principal reliance was on a body of mercenaries, who had been raised for him in Greece by various private adventurers; the chief of them, Clearchus, a Spartan exile. His Grecian soldiers amounted altogether to about ten thousand men ; and in the third year after his father's death,[7] he set forth with them and a large force of Persians to attack his brother Artaxerxes.

[1] Prideaux's "Connexion," i. p. 362. [2] B.C. 458.
[3] B.C. 445.   [4] B.C. 424.   [5] B.C. 404.
[6] Xenophon's Expedition of Cyrus the younger.
[7] B.C. 401. Xen. u s.

Had Cyrus acquainted his Greek soldiers with the object of his expedition, they would have refused to follow him in a march of three months into the heart of Asia; but, by pretending friendship to his brother, who had continued him in his command, and by professing that his purpose was to attack a neighbouring satrap, he led them on till to retreat was as difficult as to advance. At Cunaxa, in the plains of Assyria, they were met by the Persian king, whose countless host fled almost without a blow before the well-disciplined attack of the Greeks. But, though victorious in their part of the field, they lost the assistance of Cyrus, who was slain while engaging hand to hand with his brother. They soon found their situation in the highest degree critical; for, on the death of Cyrus, they were speedily forsaken by their Persian allies; and on a vast plain, shut in by unfordable rivers,—the Tigris on one side, and the Euphrates on the other,—ill supplied with provisions, and without horse or light troops,—a retreat in presence of the countless cavalry of Persia seemed almost impossible. But they were Greeks; they were strong in their discipline, and in the confidence that they were the conquering nation; and when Artaxerxes demanded that they should lay down their weapons, they bade him "come and take them;" adding, "what have soldiers left, when they lay down their arms?"

The Persians felt the presence of their natural victors; but, unwilling that this small body of men should return from the heart of Asia to proclaim their weakness, they resolved to make treachery supply the place of strength. A truce was made, which allowed them a safe return; and Tissaphernes, who succeeded Cyrus in his satrapy, undertook to guide them to their own country. Under pretence of avoiding the desert in the neighbourhood of the Euphrates, they were led to the east of the river Tigris, and their officers, invited by Tissaphernes to a friendly conference, were arrested and slain. Thus deprived of their leaders, they might probably have been dispersed by the attack which next morning he meditated against them, had not their resolution been roused by Xenophon, a young Athenian, trained in the ennobling school of Socrates, who had hitherto served among them as a private soldier. His wisdom and courage now secured that retreat which his pen afterwards immortalised. Electing him and other leaders, the ten thousand (so they were afterwards called) retreated along the eastern banks of the Tigris, till they reached the mountains from which it proceeded. Here their well-ordered discipline prevailed over the hardy valour of the Carduchian mountaineers, whom the vast armies of Persia had been unable to conquer. The great king, who paid tribute, even when he passed from Susa to Ecbatana, to the inhabitants of the highland passes which lay between, did not attempt to follow them into this wild region. On emerging from it, they entered Armenia; and, after many hardships, approached the south-eastern border of the Euxine Sea. The army was ascending the mountain, when the rear-guard perceived an unusual delay; and Xenophon pressing forward to ascertain the cause, heard the welcome shout, "The sea, the sea!" They soon reached the Grecian colony of Trapezus; and of ten thousand men who had left Cunaxa, eight thousand six hundred were found to have returned.

This celebrated expedition of the younger Cyrus, and still more the retreat of the ten thousand, revealed the weakness of Persia; and Agesilaus, the Spartan king, who soon afterwards commanded in Asia Minor against Tissaphernes, thought the time already come for its conquest.[1] But his schemes were frustrated by those divisions among his countrymen, which were excited as well by Persian gold as by Spartan arrogance. And Lacedæmon had not long profited by its victory over Athens, before there arose against it a new enemy, by which its hope of dominion was finally ex-

[1] Xenoph. "Hellenics," iv. &c.

tinguished. Thebes had hitherto taken but an inferior part in Grecian counsels, though Bœotia, of which it was the capital, was important both in size and population. But under the leading of Pelopidas, and still more of Epaminondas, it rose to sudden though transient distinction.[1] Epaminondas, the greatest military genius whom Greece had yet known, conceived the project of concentrating his force, and thus bringing it to bear on one particular point of the opposing army. The success of his plan required the adoption of various measures, by which the attention of the rest of the hostile force was distracted; while the decision of the contest was made to depend on that single point in which his force was collected. This grand design, which Alexander afterwards practised on the great scale in the fields of Asia, enabled Epaminondas to gain the first victory which had ever been attained on equal terms over the Spartan forces.[2] His success at Leuctra, in Bœotia, dissolved the charm which had heretofore enabled them to hold Peloponnesus in subjection;[3] he soon found himself at the head of the great mass of the Arcadians; he ravaged the territory of Laconia, which had never before beheld an enemy; and, as a lasting overthrow of their greatness, he restored the Messenians, whom, more than three centuries before, the Lacedæmonians had either driven into exile, or reduced to slavery. Finally, after another invasion of Laconia,[4] Epaminondas fell in a second great victory at Mantinæa, by which the strength of Sparta was finally crippled. But with him fell the ascendency of Thebes; and the last hope expired that there should arise any among the petty states of Greece which should realise the promise of its expected empire.

[1] Xenoph. "Hellenics," vi. 4, &c. Diodorus, xv. 6.
[2] B.C. 371. [3] B.C. 369. [4] B.C. 362.

DEVELOPMENT OF THE THIRD EMPIRE—ALEXANDER THE GREAT.

Philip of Macedon—Alexander—Daniel's Prophecy—Invasion of Asia—Battle of Granicus—Issus—Tyre Taken—Arbela —Bactria and India Invaded—Alexander's Plans and Death.

> "They drove the Mede and Bactrian from the field,
> And taught aspiring Babylon to yield."
>
> ROWE'S *Lucan,* viii.

THE time was now come when the harvest of victory, for which there had been so long a preparation, was finally to be reaped in the fields of Asia. The weakness of Persia and the strength of Greece,—Spartan discipline and Athenian energy,—the experience of Xenophon and the genius of Epaminondas, were all to have their effect. During the ascendency of Thebes, Pelopidas, who had been called to arbitrate some differences in the north of Greece, had brought home with him as a hostage a younger brother of the Macedonian king, named Philip.[1] In Thebes, under the teaching of Epaminondas, this prince learnt those lessons in the arts both of war and peace which enabled him, when he afterwards succeeded to the throne of Macedon,[2] to raise himself from the ruler of a semi-barbarous horde to the chief place among the Greeks. The Macedonians, a people of mixed origin, but governed by a Grecian family which claimed descent from Hercules, had hitherto exercised little influence over their southern neighbours. But Philip, steadily using every method both of force and artifice, increased his own limits, and speedily gained a party among the Grecian states. He was opposed by the Athenian orator Demosthenes, who, by his celebrated Philippics, excited the Greeks to resistance, and long delayed the establishment of Philip's authority; but this great master of eloquence did not gain sufficient confidence

---

[1] Plutarch's "Pelopidas.' Diodorus, xvi. 1, &c.   [2] B.C. 359.

for his own motives, nor did sufficient public spirit prevail in his country, to make permanent opposition to the Macedonian power. Under pretence of punishing the Phocians, who had plundered the temple of Delphi, Philip obtained a place in the Amphictyonic council,[1] which professed to represent the whole Grecian name; and by a subsequent assembly at the Isthmus of Corinth [2] he was appointed generalissimo against Persia, and every Grecian state except Sparta promised its contingent of troops. Meanwhile he had introduced the Grecian discipline among his native subjects, and the Macedonian phalanx, framed on the principles of Epaminondas, was become the most formidable body of troops in the world.

Just at this moment Philip was assassinated out of private revenge, and bequeathed the execution of his designs to his more celebrated son. In Alexander the Great all the energy which marked the Greek character was united to a power such as no Greek had heretofore possessed; while the advantages of his birth gave him those habits of superiority which were so well supported by the native pre-eminence of his mind. His father had entrusted his education to the celebrated philosopher Aristotle, who established an intellectual empire more lasting than that of his pupil; and from him Alexander acquired that ardent love of knowledge, and those enlarged views of things, which raised him above ordinary conquerors, and made his empire so important a stage in the advance of civilisation. He was passionately fond of the Greek poets, and anxious to display all the characteristics both of mind and body which they had attributed to the heroic character. Lysimachus, the instructor of his earlier boyhood, gained his heart by giving him the name of the hero of the Iliad;[3] Alexander he called Achilles; himself Phœnix, the tutor of the conqueror of Troy. When he was but young, a horse was brought to Philip's palace so high-spirited that none could

[1] B.C. 338.   [2] B.C. 338.   [3] Plutarch's "Alexander."

manage it. But this animal, Bucephalus, was subdued by Alexander, who afterwards used it in the battles in which he conquered men. When his father's court was visited by some Persian ambassadors, instead of childish questions, his inquiries respected the civil and military state of the East, its distance from his native country, and other topics, which shewed the great schemes which already occupied his mind.

And now came the fulfilment of Daniel's words, "A mighty king shall stand up, that shall rule with great dominion, and do according to his will."[1] His conquests are thus described: "An he-goat came from the west on the face of the whole earth, and touched not the ground: and the goat had a notable horn between his eyes. And he came to the ram that had two horns [the kingdom of the Medes and Persians]; and he was moved with choler against him, and smote the ram, and brake his two horns: and there was no power in the ram to stand before him, but he cast him down to the ground, and stamped upon him: and there was none that could deliver the ram out of his hand."[2]

It was to the rapidity here described that Alexander owed his success. Memnon, a Greek of talents and fidelity, was entrusted by Darius Codomanus, who now governed Persia, with the command of Asia Minor. He purposed by Persian gold to excite a general rising throughout Greece, so soon as Alexander's forces were withdrawn from it. But the young king entering Asia in the first year of his reign defeated the Persians at the passage of the Granicus,[3] and gained the whole of Asia Minor. One year more, and he gained a still greater victory at Issus in the passes of Cilicia; and, turning southward, subdued the cities of Phœnicia. By their conquest he shut out the Persians from intercourse with Greece, and thus secured himself from attack while he marched into the provinces beyond the Euphrates. He

[1] Dan. xi. 3. [2] Dan. viii. 5-7. [3] Diod. xvii. 1, &c. Arrian. i., &c.

met with little opposition in his progress till he summoned the fortress of Tyre. The ancient city, which had been so long besieged by Nebuchadnezzar, he found inhabited, but without fortifications; but the new city, which stood upon an island half a mile from shore, for a long time defied his attacks. Yet to march inland, leaving the sea under the control of the enemy, who might readily work upon the mutable spirit of the Greeks, was impossible: with great labour, therefore, he made a mound from the shore by which he purposed to reach this strongly fortified island: but the inhabitants, issuing in their ships, destroyed his works when half completed. At length he raised a fleet from the adjoining cities, and, having gained the command of the sea, he captured this mistress of the waters. Tyre has never since recovered its importance, and remains, as Ezekiel prophesied, an isthmus, where the fisherman dries his nets; the mole which Alexander constructed having joined it permanently to the continent. Its fall was not owing merely to the severities with which at the time he visited its long resistance, but to the influence of the more successful rival which he raised against it. Egypt had hitherto been in great measure closed against mercantile activity; but when Alexander entered it after the conquest of Phœnicia, he perceived, with his accustomed sagacity, what advantages were offered for commerce by the mouth of the Nile. In this spot, the key of Egypt, communicating with the East through the Red Sea and sending its fleets to the utmost west, he founded the Grecian colony which bore his name. The result justified the foresight of Aristotle's disciple, and Alexandria succeeded to the wealth of Tyre, as it afterwards did to the literary renown of Athens.

The conquest of Egypt and Phœnicia rendered it safe to attack the Persian monarch in the heart of the East. Darius had gathered an immense army of nine hundred thousand men; a large part being drawn from the brave and hardy tribes eastward of the Caspian, who, as far as the

Jaxartes, acknowledged the Persian sway. With these he occupied a vast plain in the neighbourhood of Arbela. Alexander's army consisted but of forty thousand foot and seven thousand horsemen; but they were Greeks, and their general had been trained in the institutions of Epaminondas. Alexander slept soundly the night before the battle; and his success was as complete as in his former contests. He now received the submission of Assyria; he took possession of Babylon and Persepolis; and then followed Darius, who though he had retreated through the Caspian gates into Bactria, found his traces still followed by the "leopard who had upon its back four wings of a fowl."[1] Darius was soon afterwards murdered by Bessus, satrap of Bactria, who had hoped to win Alexander's favour, but on whom he revenged the quarrel of royalty. His own conduct towards the captive wife and family of Darius had been generous and kind. After subduing Bactria, and advancing even into the Scythian desert, he turned southward to the conquest of India. He had passed the Indus, when, on the banks of the Hyphasis, one of its tributary streams, his Macedonian soldiers refused to follow him further from their native west. Alexander wept that his plans of conquest were bounded; but immediately turning towards the other designs which his vast spirit had conceived, he prepared a fleet, which sailed down the Indus under the conduct of Nearchus, and explored the passage to the Persian gulf. There Alexander again met it, and proceeding to Babylon, he commenced the great work of cementing the empire which he had so hastily composed. His object was to combine together the natives of the East and West, and to elevate the character of his Persian subjects by the infusion of Grecian discipline and vigour. Amidst his extended plans for the discovery and civilisation of the East, he saw the commercial advantages which the situation of Babylon afforded, and fixed upon it as the capital of his

[1] Dan. vii. 6.

empire. His first care was to restore the navigation of the Euphrates, which the Persians had either hindered or neglected. But in the midst of his vast projects, and of the festivities which attended his return, the conqueror of Asia was suddenly arrested by the stroke of death.

And now was accomplished the remainder of Daniel's prophecy: "The he-goat waxed very great: and when he was strong, the great horn was broken; and for it came up four notable ones towards the four winds of heaven"[1] He died of a fever, increased, if not occasioned, by intemperance. Thus was Alexander cut off after a reign of twelve years;[2] and the great empire which he had raised so quickly, was as speedily divided.

---o---

ALEXANDER'S SUCCESSORS.

The "four notable Horns"—Jews—Septuagint—Antiochus— Epiphanes—Maccabees—Antiochus stopped by the Romans.

> "Know, therefore, when my season comes to sit
> On David's throne, it shall be like a tree
> Spreading and evershadowing all the earth."— MILTON.

THE empire of Alexander was divided among his generals, who strove with various fortune for the vacant inheritance. At length the great battle of Ipsus led to the establishment of four separate kingdoms—that of Macedon, under Cassander; that of Lysimachus in Thrace and Asia Minor; that of Ptolemy in Egypt; and that of the East under the Seleucidæ. The two last were not only in themselves the most important, but require most notice in the history of the world, because to one or other of them the Jewish people continued to be subject.

[1] Dan. viii. 8.   [2] B.C. 323.

As the time drew nearer for that spiritual kingdom which was to arise out of Judæa, the influence of the Jewish people increased. Their intercourse with other nations was augmented by the settlement of a large colony at Alexandria, the seat of traffic, whence they spread into the west. Thus were the temporal plans of Alexander made subservient to the purposes of God. For the sake of this colony the Jewish Scriptures were translated into the Greek language, and attention was drawn to them by their introduction into the great library formed by King Ptolemy at Alexandria. This translation, called the Septuagint, from the number of persons [seventy-two] who were said to be employed upon it, made the Gentiles acquainted with the predictions of that universal empire which was shortly to arise out of Judæa.[1] The time which Daniel had fixed for its approach was now at hand; and the Jewish Church was able to explain the purpose and nature of these predictions with a clearness, which to a stranger the words themselves might hardly convey. Whether their meaning had been handed down by the prophets, or in whatever way it pleased God to enlighten His Church, certain it is that the books written after the volume of the Old Testament was finished, and which were called Apocrypha,* or hidden, because not part of the Church's public teaching, shew that the future hopes of mankind, and the redemption through the Word of God,[2] were familiar to faithful Israelites.[3]

Among the apocryphal writings are found the books of Maccabees, which relate how the Jews defended themselves against a tyrannical prince of the family of the Seleucidæ, named Antiochus Epiphanes.[4] They had been kindly

---

[1] Tacitus, Hist. v. 13.

[2] Targum of Jerusalem on Gen. xlix. 18. "I wait not for the deliverance of Samson or Gideon, but for the redemption through Thy Word."

[3] Ecclesiasticus i. 5; Wisdom vii. 25; Baruch iii. 37.   [4] B.C. 170.

* No student of the Apocryphal books can fail to be struck by the advance towards Christian modes of thought and expression displayed

treated by Alexander the Great; and received from him so many privileges, that Josephus, the Jewish historian, refers them to the effect of a vision which Alexander had seen before he left home, and in which a person who resembled the Jewish high priest encouraged him to his expedition. Alexander's successors likewise had favoured them, and settled them in various parts of their dominions.[1] But Antiochus Epiphanes sought the destruction of their nation and worship, as though he would have prevented the establishment of that spiritual empire for which these were making provision. Not that Antiochus, more than worldly men in general, had any especial desire for the injury of the Church; but the measures which were essential to its being, interfered with those worldly plans which he thought more important. If the Jewish system, which now seemed to hang by a thread, was done away, where would have been the spiritual preparation for Messiah's kingdom? But what was this to the Grecian monarch, when he found that his empire was weakened by the prejudices which it involved? He found the Jews a separate people in the midst of the nations; and in order to amalgamate them with his other subjects, he determined to overthrow whatever was peculiar in their institutions. Religion he saw to be the basis of them all; and as the first step, therefore, in *grecising* the Jewish people, he required them to renounce their faith. This is that "vile person," of whom Daniel prophesies in

---

[1] Josephus, xii. 3.

in them, and the longing for the "Wisdom" or "Word" of God there manifested. The Jewish Philosopher Philo, of Alexandria, touched with one hand the schools of the Platonists, while with the other he held fast by the Scriptures of the Jewish Church; and about the Christian era shewed how the two streams of thought might be brought and blended together. Thus as all nations were united in the Roman empire, as shewn later, to form a Unity in which the Church Catholic might grow, so the philosophic schools had points of union, through which they might pour their wealth of speculation and enquiry into the Treasury of the Church of Christ.

his eleventh chapter, who shall not "regard the God of his fathers, nor the desire of women, nor regard any God; for he shall magnify himself above all."[1] Against him God raised up a brave family, called the Maccabees, from the title of their first leader, who, because he broke in pieces all opposition, was called the Hammerer[2] (Maccabæus). By this family the Jewish nation was preserved when it seemed in the utmost danger; they maintained the peculiarity of its distinctive institutions; and thus was fulfilled the prophecy of God, that it should continue to be a separate people till the coming of our Lord. "The sceptre shall not depart from Judah, nor a lawgiver from between his feet, until Shiloh come."[3]

The predictions of the prophet Daniel concerning Antiochus Epiphanes and the Jews who contended for the preservation of their Church and nation, have probably a further meaning, and describe the fate of Christ's Church and its enemies in after-times. Antiochus is but a type of every carnal ruler who sacrifices the Church because he finds it in his way in the attainment of earthly greatness. Yet these predictions depict exactly the conduct of this tyrannous king, and of the valiant Maccabees: "Arms shall stand on his part, and they shall pollute the sanctuary of strength, and shall take away the daily sacrifice, and they shall place the abomination that maketh desolate. And such as do wickedly against the covenant shall he corrupt by flatteries: but the people that do know their God shall be strong, and do exploits."[4] And one remarkable circumstance in the king's life is set forth in the same chapter; a circumstance which marks the introduction into the East of that fourth great empire which was shortly to become predominant.[5] Antiochus invaded Egypt, and, by adding

---

[1] Dan. xi. 37.
[2] Maccabæus was a personal name. Compare Josephus, xii. 8, and 1 Macc. ii. 66.
[3] Gen. xlix. 10.
[4] Dan. xi. 31-32.
[5] B.C. 168.

it to his other territories, would have increased his power of crushing the Jews. But at that moment, says Daniel, "the ships of Chittim," *i.e.*, of Europe, "shall come against him; therefore he shall be grieved and return."[1] This return was occasioned by the threats of certain Roman ambassadors, who, landing from their ships, met him close to Alexandria in Egypt. The strength and pride of that fourth iron empire was seen in its ambassador. King Antiochus, who had been at Rome, knew and spoke to him as a friend. "No private friendship till our business is completed," said the ambassador, and gave him certain letters which he brought from Rome, requiring him to quit Egypt. "I will consider of them," said the king, when he had read them, "and give an answer." The Roman, drawing a circle round the king with his staff in the sandy soil, said, "Before you quit this circle, you shall give me my answer to the Roman senate." The king replied that he would obey its wishes.[2] And thus appears upon the scene that fourth empire of which Daniel had spoken: "A fourth beast, dreadful and terrible, and strong exceedingly; and it had great iron teeth: it devoured and brake in pieces, and stamped the residue with the feet of it: and it was diverse from all the beasts that were before it."[3]

[1] Dan. xi. 30.   [2] Livy, xlv. 12.   [3] Dan. vii. 7.

ROMAN, OR FOURTH GREAT EMPIRE.

ROMAN, OR FOURTH GREAT EMPIRE.

Early Constitution—Patricians—Plebeians—Invasion of Gaul—Punic Wars—Hannibal—Wars with Alexander's Successors—Roman Character Impaired—Gracchi—Marius—Sylla—Pompey—Julius Cæsar—Augustus—Universal Empire—Peace Throughout the Roman World.

"The Persians at one time acquired great power and dominion; but as often as they ventured to pass the limits of Asia, not only their empire but their existence was endangered. The Lacedæmonians having contended long for the mastery of Greece, could scarcely retain it without dispute for twelve years. The Macedonians ruled Europe from the Adriatic to the Danube; and afterwards having overthrown the Persians, acquired the empire of Asia. Yet even they, though their power seemed to be most extensive and matured, left the larger part of the world wholly unsubdued. For Sicily, and Sardinia, and Libya, they never ventured to attack; and with the most warlike nations of western Europe they were scarcely acquainted. But the Romans, having reduced not a part, but well nigh the whole of the inhabited earth, have acquired a power such as their contemporaries may envy, and their successors can never surpass."—POLYBIUS, i. 2.

THE Roman empire was diverse from all that went before it; because while they were governed by kings, it had grown up under comparatively free institutions, and under a council of elders called the senate. The other empires had belonged to powerful nations, but this to a great city, "which reigned over the kings of the earth."[1]

The city of Rome had been built seven hundred and fifty-three years before Christ, a little previous to the time when the ten tribes were carried captive by Shalmanezer. The fables which prevailed respecting its origin, shew an

[1] Rev. xvii. 18.

early anticipation of its future greatness. A head,[1] we are told, was found in digging its foundations, in token that it should be the head of the world; and a wolf, which suckled its founder Romulus, prefigured the fierce and conquering character of its citizens. Its early government was kingly; and seven persons are named as having in succession worn the crown—Romulus, Numa Pompilius, Tullus Hostilius, Ancus Martius, Tarquinius Priscus, Servius Tullius, and Tarquinius Superbus.

Servius Tullius had afterwards the character of having devised institutions somewhat resembling those of Solon,[2] by which the different classes of citizens were to be united, and a measure of power placed in the hands of the people. But his measures were undone by his successor Tarquinius Superbus (the Proud), whose tyranny made the kingly name hateful to the Romans. Yet his oppressions might have been borne in silence, had not the insult offered by his son Sextus to Lucretia, the wife of Collatinus, given occasion to an outbreak of popular feeling. More susceptible of insults than of injuries, the people rose under Brutus; and after banishing the Tarquins, declared that the name of king should never again be endured at Rome. Two consuls were appointed, to whom the executive part of the kingly office was yearly committed; for times of great emergency a dictator was named, who possessed likewise for a season that legislative power which belonged in common to the senate and the people. But soon after the expulsion of the kings, it became matter of fierce dispute, of what class the assembly of the people should be composed. The Patricians, or descendants of those who had followed Romulus, refused to admit the Plebeians, or subsequent settlers, to any share in the government. The absence of political power involved the suffering of

[1] Livy, i. 56; Dionysius, iv. The early prevalence of the story of the wolf is shewn by the antiquity of its statue.
[2] Livy, i. 42, &c

personal injury, until the Plebeians, by threatening a total secession from Rome, obtained their own magistrates, the tribunes, as defenders of their rights. Under their guidance they advanced from step to step, till they gradually gained admission to all the privileges of the old inhabitants.

Meanwhile Rome was winning its way to power over its neighbours; though it received a rude shock when a tribe of Gauls from the north of Italy seized and burned the city,[1] and remained for some time masters of all but the capitol. They were driven back by Camillus; or, as the more accurate Polybius tells us,[2] retreated voluntarily on hearing that their own country was invaded by the Veneti. And before their next incursion, the Romans had so completely united the various Latin tribes as to be secure from their attacks. In the first five centuries after the founding of their city, all the southern nations of Italy had submitted to their influence, while their domestic disputes were allayed by the admission of the plebeians to every office. Rome still continued to be an aristocratic state; for the senate and consuls possessed much of the legislative, and almost all the executive, power; and the principle of Solon's institution was strictly followed, by which a qualification was required for office; but no distinction of races divided the state, and the jealousy had passed away between the first settlers and those who had risen up around them.

At this period Rome came into collision with a rival republic, which long disputed with it the empire of the world. Carthage, on the southern shore of the Mediterranean, of earlier origin than Rome, of greater wealth, of more extended alliances,— was the only state which promised to check its rising greatness; and these two commonwealths seemed set over against one another in order to determine whether the race of Japheth or the family of Ham should possess the empire of the west.

---

[1] B.C. 390. [2] Polyb. ii. 18.

Like its Phœnician parent, Carthage had found that the inhabitants of Italy did not admit of its ascendency; and an early treaty with Rome shews not only its commercial greatness, but the strength and hardihood of the Italians.[1] But in Spain Carthage had acquired immense influence; she ruled the north of Africa and the islands of the Mediterranean; and it was obvious that nothing but the power of Rome could prevent her from gaining the mastery over the European nations.

In the first Punic war—so called from the Latin name given to the Carthaginians from their Phœnician descent—Sicily was the prize for which the two cities contended;[2] and Rome, after obtaining the dominion of the sea, prevailed over her rival. Hence a deep hostility in the breasts of the Carthaginians. Amilchar, their most celebrated general, passed into Spain, and spent nine years in strengthening and extending the Carthaginian power in that country, that he might afterwards turn the force thus gained against Italy. On his death, his son Hannibal, whom he had solemnly pledged to eternal hatred against the Romans, succeeded to his forces and his enterprise. After completing his designs in Spain, Hannibal led the large army, which he had collected there and brought from Africa, across the Pyrenees into Gaul.[3] Advancing for some distance up the Rhone, he marched by unknown routes across the Alps, till, by the pass of the little St. Bernard, he entered Italy. To lead a large army, encumbered with cavalry and elephants, across these hitherto unexplored mountains, was an attempt which it required all the daring of this extraordinary man to conceive, and all his sagacity to execute. Arriving among the Gauls of Lombardy, whom the Romans had imperfectly subdued in the interval since the first Punic war, he reinforced his army; and falling upon the plains of Italy, compelled the

---

[1] B.C. 508. Polybius, iii. 22.   [2] B.C. 264. Polybius, i. 16, &c.
[3] B.C. 218. Polybius, iii. 33, &c. Livy, xxi. 21, &c.

Romans, who had heretofore fought for empire, to contend for existence. He defeated them in three great battles; in that of Cannæ they lost above fifty thousand men;[1] and at one time he even appeared under the walls of Rome. But the Romans lost nothing of their ancient confidence. While Hannibal was encamped before their gates, the land which he occupied was sold by public auction in their city. They continued to press the war in Spain, and finally carried it into Africa; while the Carthaginians, who were wanting in energy and public spirit, made but feeble efforts to aid their invincible general. At length, after maintaining his ground in Italy for fifteen years, Hannibal was compelled to return to defend his native country, confessing that the fortune of Rome prevailed over his wisest efforts; and his defeat at Zama in Africa concluded the second Punic war.[2] As the Phœnicians never came into collision with the Greeks without feeling their inferiority, so was Carthage compelled to yield to the ascendency of Rome.

The contest with Carthage had long been waged with doubtful or inconsiderable success. But this enemy once removed, the Roman arms spread like a torrent over the earth. Within ten years they had invaded Macedon, and gained a signal victory over its king, Philip;[3] they had defeated Antiochus,[4] who ruled over the eastern division of what had been Alexander's empire, and were received as the sovereign arbitrators of every dispute both in Asia Minor and in Greece. At first, however, they were content to extend their influence without enlarging their dominions; and while they were viewed as formidable neighbours by the kings of Macedon and the East, they entered into friendly alliance with the smaller states,—Pergamus, which was ruled by Attalus; and Rhodes, which had become the chief emporium of Grecian commerce. But in a few years their designs became more manifest. Perseus, son of Philip

---

[1] B.C. 216. [2] B.C. 201. [3] B.C. 197. Livy, xxxiii. 8, &c.
[4] B.C. 190. Livy, xxxvii.

king of Macedon, was defeated and dethroned in the second Macedonian war;[1] and after being left for a time in independence, Macedon itself was reduced to a Roman province. At the same time, Corinth and Carthage were destroyed;[2] and Greece, which had hitherto been allowed the show of liberty, became dependent. Spain likewise was conquered; while the kingdom of the friendly Attalus was gained by inheritance.

And thus that spectacle was exhibited which Daniel had long before discerned with the eye of prophecy. To "devour,"[3] to "tread down," and to "break in pieces," was exactly Rome's office among the nations. Every thing must bend and yield to the iron sceptre of its sway. Beforetime the aspect of the world had been diversified. There were republics in Europe, and monarchies in Asia; the East had her cavalry, the West her foot-soldiers; some cities were enriched by commerce, others distinguished for arts and arms. But now all was frozen up in the cold uniformity of this iron empire. The old forms, whether of empire or freedom, were trampled under foot and forgotten. The mistress of the world sent forth her prætors and proconsuls to rule instead of kings; she spread abroad her colonies to be a model and rule for cities; she imposed her laws and customs on nations the most dissimilar; and so "dreadful and terrible" was she, that none might gainsay her. Vast roads, uniform and unbending, were the tracks which she made for herself through the world, that so the most inaccessible countries might be laid open to her armies; and in making them, she hewed through mountains and filled up valleys, as though the earth was as subject to her as its inhabitants.

Nor was the private character of her citizens less stern and masterful than their public deeds. To all that refines and humanises life, to the arts and literature, they were indifferent; and of those Latin writers who rose up after

---

[1] B.C. 168. Livy, xliv. &c. [2] B.C. 146. [3] Dan. vii. 23.

the fall of their republic, the most distinguished were formed on Greek models, and had little that was Roman about them, except the name. Everything was swallowed up by the desire of pre-eminence: they were neither kindly nor generous; toward strangers they were proud, overbearing, and intolerant; among themselves fierce, cruel, and relentless. Their meanest officers behaved with arrogance and insolence to the greatest princes of the earth, and took pleasure in shewing their contempt for the manners and feelings of other nations.

But now a great change befell the mistress of the world. Without abandoning her pride and fierceness, she began to lose those virtues which had originally given her power to display them. The subjugation of these rich and extended provinces was fatal to the conquerors.[1] The ascendency of the Romans had resulted from their extraordinary reverence for those natural principles of right which, being derived from the early notions of men's duty to God, had lingered in the recollection of untutored nations. "Among the Greeks," says their countryman Polybius, "though a man be bound by ten bonds, and twice as many witnesses, he cannot be induced to keep faith, if he be trusted with a single talent of public money; whereas the Romans, when during office or embassy they have a large sum in their hands, are held to their duty by the mere sanction of an oath. So that whereas among others you can hardly find a man who abstains from plundering the public, among the Romans such a crime is rarely heard of."[2] And this purity he attributes to their ancient habits of piety and respect for an unwritten law.

To this cause of the greatness of the republic must be added another circumstance — that singular confidence in the genius of Rome which had led its senate, when the consul Varro returned almost alone from the defeat at Cannæ, to render him public thanks, "because he had not

---

[1] Livy, xxxix. 7, &c.   [2] Polybius, vi. 56.

despaired of the republic."[1] The patriotism of the Romans was not, like that of Sparta, the forced effect of an education inapplicable under the ordinary circumstances of life; it was the natural produce of the domestic virtues. With the energy of freedom was blended a discretion which gave its leaders confidence in themselves, and an unconquerable conviction that they were citizens of a state destined to be the head of the world. To what but a divine Providence can we refer this conviction, when we find it harmonise with a prophecy which had been uttered centuries before in another quarter of the globe—thus realising in Europe what had been predicted in Asia?

But the virtues of the Roman character began now to be impaired. On the conquest of Greece the seed of public spirit was speedily corrupted by the Epicurean philosophy. The opportunities of wealth, which the leading citizens derived from high commands, enabled them to put into effect what this base system recommended. And so soon as those in power were seen to grow wealthy from their rule over the provinces, a new series of disputes convulsed the state. It was no longer between races who aimed at equal rights, but between the wealthy who sought to keep, and the needy who strove to share their possessions. Hence the distinction of the ancient free states—that public were preferred to private ends—was lost. The history of Rome, from the establishment of its foreign power till it sank under the dominion of the Cæsars, is but a catalogue of conspiracies, seditions, and civil wars; and the inward spectacle of this fourth kingdom almost resembles the confusion of Babel, when the first project of universal empire was discomfited by God.

The earliest of these civil dissensions was excited by two brothers, named Tiberius[2] and Caius Gracchus,[3] who successively demanded a division of those vast spoils which had of late years been acquired by Rome. Their project of an

---

[1] Livy, xxii. 61.   [2] B.C. 133.   [3] B.C. 121. Plutarch's Gracchi.

agrarian law was evaded by the senate, and they perished themselves in the disturbances which they occasioned; but they were able to commit the judicial power to the knights, a body whom they aimed at rendering a counterpoise to the senate.

The Gracchi were soon followed by a demagogue of a different class in Marius,[1] the conqueror of Jugurtha,—a successful general, whose services were thought so needful that he was four times elected consul, when Rome was threatened by the barbarian Cimbri,[2] whose path had been marked by devastation from the Euxine to the Po. Marius struck a powerful blow at the ancient system, by admitting the lowest class of the people to the regular service of the legions. In such a turbulent state as Rome then presented, political power must soon follow military strength. Marius set the example of occupying the city by force, as though it had been a hostile capital; and indulged his hatred by the massacre of his opponents. But the lesson which he had given to others was soon read to himself. Sylla, a warm adherent of the aristocratical party, returned shortly from the East with the army which had triumphed over Mithridates,[3] king of Pontus, the last and greatest foreign enemy of the republic. With more power than Marius, he made a proscription of his opponents—set forth, that is, a list of those whom he desired to destroy; and, after being appointed perpetual dictator, and abolishing the tribunitial power, he gave to the party of the senate what seemed a lasting authority. Lucullus, Pompey, Crassus, the distinguished men of the next generation, arose out of his party. But Pompey, finding the senate unwilling to gratify those exorbitant demands to which he thought that his military successes entitled him, restored the tribunitial power,[4] and by its aid gained an excess of greatness inconsistent with the situation of a private citizen. The senate

---

[1] Plutarch's Lives of Marius, Sylla, Cæsar, &c.   B.C. 106.
[2] B.C. 101.   [3] B.C. 82.   [4] B.C. 70.

at this time was not wanting in great men; and its authority was especially maintained by Cicero, the first Roman who had risen without military talents to first-rate distinction. But Cicero had neither influence nor strength of character to wrestle with the military leaders of his day. After a temporary banishment, he submitted without opposition to what was called the triumvirate.[1] This was a combination of three persons, Pompey, Crassus, and Cæsar, who had sufficient power to rule the senate at their will, and to apportion among themselves and their followers the offices of government. Pompey had now returned from the East, where he had finally destroyed the kingdom of Mithridates, and decided respecting the destiny of its various states. It was at this time that he was called in by Hyrcanus, one of the Maccabæan princes, who was besieging his brother in Jerusalem, and by Pompey's assistance gained the government. The heroic days of the Maccabees were now passed; and Antipater, the Idumæan, father of Herod, who was at present an adherent of Hyrcanus, was shortly afterwards made ruler of Judæa by the Romans. Pompey had administered the affairs of the East with all the authority of an absolute monarch; but the designs of the triumvirate were found to turn exclusively to Cæsar's profit. Better fitted than Pompey for a popular leader, the reputed successor of the party of Marius, Cæsar gained the command of the province of Gaul, and there and in Britain he trained his army to conquests, of which his own country was the last victim. Pompey at length found it necessary[2] to throw himself upon the senate; and Crassus, their associate, having perished in an expedition against Parthia, the empire of the world was contested between these two leaders. With Pompey sided the senate and the aristocratical party; men of broken fortunes and of turbulent minds wished success to Cæsar. They met in the plains of Pharsalia;[3] and the legions of Cæsar, trained in the hardships of the Gallic war, proved

[1] B.C. 60.   [2] B.C. 50.   [3] B.C. 48.

too powerful for the troops which Pompey had collected from the more tranquil portions of the empire.

Cæsar had now gained the summit of his ambition, but not with any purpose of restoring the ancient system, or resigning, as Sylla had done, his unconstitutional authority. Democracy had now run its course, and ended, according to its natural progress, in absolute power. No other system could longer suffice for the government of Rome. Even when Cæsar had fallen by the daggers of Brutus and Cassius,[1] a new triumvirate was speedily formed by Antony, Octavius, and Lepidus. Hence fresh proscriptions, and a new war for the empire of the world. At length Antony, being defeated in the battle of Actium, Augustus succeeded to the supreme command,[2] though out of respect for ancient prejudices he declined the name of king, and adopted the title of emperor, which it had been usual for every Roman general to bear when he returned victorious from a field of battle.

And now the world began to present a very different appearance from anything which had been seen within the recollection of man. None of the three preceding empires had filled the earth so completely as did the Roman. The power of none seemed to be so well compacted. The Romans, who had never been a year at peace since their city was built, were now free from all enemies; and the temple of Janus, which it was their custom to open whenever they went to war, was for the first time permanently closed. Mankind began to look with wonder on what should follow this new state of things. A contemporary heathen historian[3] expresses his surprise at seeing the whole destiny of the tribes of men thus gathered into a single channel, and ready to expand itself into some unwonted form.

The general extension of the Greek language throughout the East co-operated with this universal outspread of the

---

[1] B.C. 44. [2] B.C. 31. [3] Polybius, i. 3.

Roman power. The truths which had been gathered from the Old Testament worked among the heathen. An universal empire—a reign of peace—the deliverance of mankind,—these they knew were expected. Hence the Roman poet Virgil predicts the birth of one who should bring back the auspicious era of ancient innocence and plenty.

> " The jarring nations He in peace shall bind,
> And with paternal virtues rule mankind;
> Unbidden earth shall wreathing ivy bring,
> And fragrant herbs (the promises of spring),
> As her first offerings to her infant King;
> The goats with strutting dugs shall homeward speed,
> And lowing herds secure from lions feed;
> His cradle shall with rising flowers be crowned;
> The serpent's brood shall die; the sacred ground
> Shall weeds and poisonous plants refuse to bear;
> Each common bush shall Syrian roses wear.
>   Yet of old fraud some footsteps shall remain,
> The merchant still shall plough the deep for gain;
> Great cities shall with walls be compass'd round,
> And sharpened shares shall vex the fruitful ground.
>   But when to ripen'd manhood he shall grow,
> The greedy sailor shall the seas forego;
> No boat shall cut the waves for foreign ware,
> For every soil shall every product bear."[1]

Such were men's expectations; but, as has happened in all times, they expected from the world that which was to be manifested in the Church. For they knew not the full glory of that prophecy which it has been given to us to understand: "the greaves of the warrior, his weapons, and his garments rolled in blood—these shall be a burning and fuel of fire. For unto us a child is born, unto us a son is given: and the government shall be upon His shoulder: and His name shall be called Wonderful, Counsellor, the mighty God, the everlasting Father, the Prince of Peace."[2]

---

[1] Dryden's Virgil, "Eclogue" iv.   [2] Isaiah ix. 5.

OUR LORD'S COMING. THE
KINGDOM OF HEAVEN.

OUR LORD'S COMING. THE KINGDOM OF HEAVEN.

Prophecies fulfilled—Our Lord's Birth—Wise Men—Herod—Our Lord as Prophet, Priest, and King—His Empire, wherein like the four preceding ones—Means of admission into it—Prophecies of its durability.

> "From thence, far off, he unto him did shew
>   A little path that was both steep and long,
> Which to a goodly city led his view;
>   Whose walls and towers were builded high and strong
> Of pearl and precious stone, that earthly tongue
>   Cannot describe, nor wit of man can tell;
>   Too high a ditty for my simple song:
> The city of the great King hight it well,
> Wherein eternal peace and happiness doth dwell."
> —SPENSER.

FOR whom, then, was this mighty preparation? The first part of Abraham's promise had long been realised; the second was now to be fulfilled. The appointed years of Daniel's prophecy had run their course; the desire of all nations was at hand. Jacob had predicted, that till he came the Jewish people should not cease to be a separate nation: as yet they continued under their own princes; but a little while and they must be lost, like other tribes, in the wide-sweeping wave of Roman power. Now, therefore, was the time for that which Balaam had so long before declared, "there shall come a star out of Jacob, and a sceptre shall rise out of Israel."

The men of this world are often unwitting instruments of the providence of God. In the twenty-ninth year of his reign,[1] Augustus Cæsar issued a decree, "that all the world should be taxed." As Judæa was still under its own princes, "this taxing was" not "made" there till some years afterwards, "when Cyrenius was Governor of Syria." But though the Jews as yet paid nothing, they were notwithstanding ordered to be enrolled, and an account taken of their numbers and property. Little did the proud Roman think, when he was thus making display of his power and riches, that his purpose was in truth but one link in that chain which would lead to the establishment of an empire greater and more lasting than his own.

Yet so it was. It had been predicted that at Bethlehem the Christ should be born. Now, to be taxed, every one went to his father's city. "Joseph," therefore, "went up from Galilee, out of the city of Nazareth, into Judæa, unto the city of David, which is called Bethlehem (because he was of the house and lineage of David), to be taxed with Mary his espoused wife, being great with child. And so it was, that, while they were there, the days were accomplished that she should be delivered. And she brought forth her first-born son, and wrapped him in swaddling clothes, and laid him in a manger."[2]

Thus did "the Heir"[3] come to His inheritance: "the Word was made flesh, and dwelt among us."[4] His birth was immediately known in a distant land: "the Gentiles," it had been said, "shall come to Thy light; and kings to the brightness of Thy rising."[5] By a wonderful remembrance, and a miraculous interpretation of Balaam's prediction, some distinguished persons were brought from a distant country, and offered their gifts to their infant Saviour. "Where," they said, "is He who has been born king of the Jews?" Epiphany, or the manifestation of Christ to the

---

[1] B.C. 3. The words B.C., or before Christ, mean before his third year: A.D., or anno Domini, *i.e.*, in the year of our Lord, mean after his third year.

[2] Luke ii. 4-7.   [3] Luke xx. 14.   [4] 1 John i. 14.   [5] Is. lx. 3.

Gentiles, is kept by the Church, on the twelfth day after the feast of the nativity, in memory of these "wise men," who had "seen His star in the east, and were come to worship Him."[1] Thus did it please God, by some unknown means, to spread abroad the expectation of that spiritual kingdom, which He was to establish.

Herod, who at this time was king in Judæa, though by adoption a Jew, yet having gained the throne by usurpation, was troubled at the predictions which he heard concerning this future Sovereign. He was the son of Antipater, an Idumæan, who had been an adherent of Hyrcanus the Maccabæan prince, whom Pompey had restored: Antipater had subsequently obtained the government of Judæa from Cæsar, and had left it to his son Herod. But, though Herod had secured himself by marrying Mariamne, the heiress of the Maccabæan family, yet so conscious was he of the insecurity of his power, that he put to death his own son, out of jealousy of the superior title to the throne which the boy derived from his mother.[2] This act of cruelty accords well enough with that of which he was guilty in order to destroy our Lord, when he put to death all the children in Bethlehem "from two years old and under."[3] But Joseph, warned by God in a dream, had carried our Lord into Egypt; and when he brought Him back, a year afterwards, on Herod's death, finding that Archelaus reigned in the room of his father Herod, he carried Him to his own city Nazareth. From thence, in His twelfth year,[4] our Lord went up to Jerusalem; and, according to Jewish custom, was admitted into the temple. In the same year was Archelaus dethroned by the Romans, and Judæa made a province of their empire. Thus did "the sceptre depart from Judah"[5] at that very season when Shiloh came, to whom the gathering of the nations should be.

For thirty years our Lord remained unknown at Nazareth.

---

[1] Matt. ii. 2.   [2] Joseph. Antiq. xvi. 17.   [3] Matt. ii. 16.
[4] A.D. 10.   [5] Gen xlix. 10.

When come to the age at which the Jewish ministers were ordered to begin their service,[1] at which Joseph, the ancient preserver of Israel, was raised to the government of the land of Egypt,[2] and David to the sovereignty, our Lord commenced His public ministry. It lasted during part of three years. His words and His actions—the only perfect example ever given among men—are written in those holy gospels, which are the charter of the Christian's hope. At length,[3] He "suffered under Pontius Pilate," the governor of Judæa on behalf of the Roman emperor Tiberius, who had succeeded Augustus. For our Lord's example was but one of the objects for which He lived. He was the substance of those things of which the law had "but the shadow." Whatsoever had been foretold or foredone had its reality in Him. He was the true paschal Lamb, whose blood was sprinkled for mankind's preservation. Even in His life, He "came not to be ministered unto, but to minister;"[4] but it was in His death that He "gave His life a ransom instead of many." His sacrifice upon the cross on Good Friday, the season of the Jewish passover, was the real sin-offering, "which taketh away the sin of the world."[5] The shedding of His blood was the only expiatory sacrifice.[6]

But, besides giving an example and making an atonement, our Lord came to establish an empire. Not only was He Prophet and Priest, but King. This He had begun to proclaim from the time that His forerunner, John the Baptist, was cast into prison. "From that time Jesus began to preach, and to say, Repent, for the kingdom of heaven is at hand."[7] This is that kingdom of which Daniel speaks as rising in the time of the fourth, or Roman empire: "In the days of these kings shall the God of heaven set up a kingdom, which shall never be destroyed; and the kingdom shall not be left to other people, but it shall break in pieces

---

[1] Numb. iv. 3. [2] Gen. xli. 46. [3] A.D. 31. [4] Matt. xx. 28.
[5] John i. 29. [6] Heb. x. 4, 14. [7] Matt. v. 17.

and consume all these kingdoms, and it shall stand for ever."[1] Three things are mentioned as distinguishing it: that in its rise it should be imperceptible; in its extent, unbounded; in its duration without end. And that such should be the character of His empire, our Lord declared in fuller words: it was to be a stone cut out of a mountain without hands.[2] "And when He was demanded of the Pharisees, when the kingdom of God should come, He answered them, and said, The kingdom of God cometh not with observation; neither shall they say, Lo here! or lo there! for, behold, the kingdom of God is among[3] you."[4]

This is further explained in our Lord's parables. The gradual manner in which His empire should arise is declared in the parable of the leaven: "The kingdom of heaven is like unto leaven, which a woman took, and hid in three measures of meal, till the whole was leavened."[5] His kingdom was not to be set up by any violent exercise of power, but was to grow, as knowledge or affection might spread silently through the hearts of a people. Thus might agreement extend from one family to another household, from one nation to another people. Thus did the Ninevites repent as one man at the preaching of Jonah. And thus has Christ's kingdom ever been extended, by the imperceptible growth of faith in hearts which grace has renewed.

But something more than this is needful to form a kingdom: not merely an inward spirit is required, but an outward form. "The greatness of the kingdom under the whole heaven shall be given to the people of the saints of the Most High." Besides the growth of Christian faith in the hearts of men, the prophecy of old looked to the establishment of something which, like the four pre-

---

[1] Dan. ii. 44.   [2] Dan. ii. 45.
[3] This is the marginal reading. That in the text looks to a further and deeper meaning of the same words.
[4] Luke xvii. 20, 21.   [5] Matt. ii. 33.   [6] Dan. vii. 27.

ceding empires, should be the main and central object in the world; the chief spectacle which men should behold; the mountain which should be seen to "fill the whole earth."[1] And such our Lord describes in other parables: "The kingdom of heaven is like unto a grain of mustard-seed, which indeed is the least of all seeds, but when it is grown is the greatest among herbs, and becometh a tree, so that the birds of the air come and lodge under the branches of it."[2] His kingdom, then, like those of old, is to stand forth as the chief thing of its time,—as filling the world, like those which went before it. In other places He calls it His Church. This name, which in its original means an assembly, shows that the kingdom of God is to be made up of a collection of individuals. And that these individuals were to be gathered together by some outward bond, He further taught in those parables, in which He declared that bad as well as good men should be found in the kingdom of God: "The kingdom of God is like unto a net, that was cast into the sea, and gathered of every kind."[3] It is not, therefore, mere inward faith which admits men into the kingdom of God here below—though none but the faithful profit by its blessings,—there must be some outward means which unites the Church, like the four preceding empires, into one body, and admits men of all characters into God's earthly fold.

It is probable that during the forty days which elapsed between our Lord's resurrection from the dead and His ascension into heaven, He gave His disciples more full and express instruction than they had before received, respecting those outward means by which men were to be admitted into His earthly kingdom. Certain it is that His very last injunction before His departure directed their attention to the sacrament of baptism, as the appointed method for gathering in disciples from all nations; and no sooner had they received the gift of the Holy Ghost, than the Lord's

[1] Dan. ii. 35.   [2] Matt. xiii.   [3] Matt. xiii. 47.

supper became, in like manner, a main part of their continual worship. And if baptism be the means by which men are received into the Christian congregation, by the holy eucharist their union is renewed and strengthened. We read in the Prayer-book, that those "who duly receive" it are "thereby assured that" they "are very members incorporate in the mystical body of" Christ, "which is the blessed company of all faithful people."[1] And this accords with St. Paul's saying: "We being many are one body: for we are all partakers of one bread."[2] By these two ordinances, therefore, properly received, do men become and continue members of the family of God. And as of old time soldiers called that a sacrament by which they pledged their allegiance to their leader, so are these two fitly called the SACRAMENTS,* because thereby men's part in the Church is given and confirmed. Yet we must be careful to bear in mind the truth which our article declares, that the "sacraments be not only badges of men's profession, but rather" "effectual signs of grace, by which God doth work invisibly in us."[3] If they mean something on our part, they mean something also on the part of God. Our Lord appointed them, not merely as the means whereby men might enter His kingdom, but also as the channels through which He might replenish the faithful with His grace.

Such, then, is that kingdom which our Lord founded; of which the increase was, by His spiritual presence in the hearts of His servants, given through the sacraments which He had ordained. He declared that its progress should be gradual. He taught that it should not interfere with worldly sovereignty: "My kingdom is not of this world." But as He had said that its rise should be imperceptible, so did He foretell that it should attain to all that Daniel had predicted

---

[1] Communion Service.   [2] 1 Cor. x. 17.   [3] Art. xxv.

* "Prayer is the approach of man to God, and sacrament is the going forth of God to meet man."—S. Baring Gould, "Origin and Dev. of Religious Belief," vol. i. p. 396.

in the extent and duration of its sway : " This Gospel of the kingdom shall be preached in all nations." The former empires did not so fill the earth that there was room for nothing besides. But they occupied its middle place ; their fame went into all lands. And so Christ's kingdom : it is to be everywhere witnessed. Whether it is to penetrate into every abyss, we know not ; but it is to " cover the earth, as the waters cover the sea."

And not less certain is its enduring character. Our Lord left eleven apostles, who were to be His witnesses to the end of the world. Their first act was to associate another, who, by that circumstance, gained not more individual knowledge, but that office of an apostle, by which he witnessed to the truth. To His apostles our Lord gave His final pledge, " Lo, I am with you always, even unto the end of the world." And as He is present with those who execute this office, so is this office itself a perpetual memorial of His truth. So that wheresoever men exercise a bishop's office throughout the world, they give their witness to that kingdom in which God has made them apostles.

THE APOSTLES. THE CHURCH ESTABLISHED.

Faith of the Apostles—Day of Pentecost—Gospel First Preached to Jews—Gentile Converts—Council at Jerusalem—Two Orders of Ministers besides the College of Apostles—St. James—St. Paul at Athens and Rome—Pastoral Epistles—Questions whether the Jewish System would continue—Decided by Destruction of Jerusalem — Jews banished Palestine—Meeting of Apostles in Judæa—Universal Establishment of the Order of Bishops.

> "Is not from hence the way that leadeth right
> To that most glorious house that glistereth bright
> With burning stars and ever living fire,
> Whereof the keys are to thy hand behight?"—SPENSER.

THE foundations of the Church were laid by the Lord; it was built up after His departure by His apostles. Their first act had been to complete their own body, by adding a twelfth witness to our Lord's resurrection.[1] Thus they shewed their confidence in the continuance of that system which they were called upon to administer.

But they were still ignorant of one material feature of the future dispensation. They believed the Church to be God's kingdom below; and that in it were to be fulfilled the promises of the Old Testament: but they thought it was to be built within the limits of the Jewish nation; that, to be Christians, men must first be Jews either by birth or adoption. When our Lord taught them that they were to perpetuate His Church, their question was, "Lord, wilt Thou at this time restore again the kingdom to Israel?"

Ten days after our Lord's ascension, on the Jewish feast of weeks, the apostles were endued with signal gifts of the Holy Ghost. The most apparent of these was that miraculous command of languages which aided them in extending Christ's universal kingdom, just as the miraculous confu-

---

[1] A.D. 31.

sion of tongues had defeated the universal outspread of the first worldly power. The descent of the Holy Ghost on the second of the three great Jewish feasts, as our Lord's crucifixion had taken place on the first, seemed to imply that the Mosaic system was henceforth to be hallowed to those higher purposes of which it was an emblem. But the apostles were soon taught by St. Peter's interview with the centurion Cornelius,[1] that the Gentiles also were to be brought into Christ's fold. And, shortly afterwards, it pleased God to call two more apostles, St. Paul and St. Barnabas,[2] who were set apart by the express witness of the Holy Ghost for the benefit of the heathen.

The appointment of these fresh labourers to this specific office did not take place till above thirteen years after our Lord's death;[3] and then it is that St. Paul and his companion, who had before been called teachers, are first named apostles.[4] St. Paul had already spent about eight years in more private labours, chiefly in his own country of Cilicia,[5] before he entered upon this public sphere. His present mission led to a final decision respecting the admission of Gentile converts. Paul and Barnabas, after a short visit to Cyprus, had penetrated into the heart of Asia Minor, and formed Christian communities, not only from among the scattered Jews, but from the ignorant heathen. On their return to Antioch, they stated "how God had opened the door of faith to the Gentiles."[6] Their conduct gave offence to some Jewish brethren, who maintained that though it was allowable to make heathen converts, as had been done by St. Peter, yet, that when converted, they must conform to the Jewish law.[7] A question of this kind, on which the future course of Christ's kingdom depended, required a reference, it was thought, to the collective body of apostles and elders. With this view the two new apostles went up

---

[1] A.D. 32. [2] Acts xiii. 1. [3] A.D. 45. [4] Acts xiii. 1, xiv. 14.
[5] Acts xi. 25, xv. 41. [6] Acts xiv. 27. [7] Acts xv. 2.

to Jerusalem.[1] The occasion was of most memorable interest, not only because it so deeply affected the probable extent of the Christian community, but also because this great council was attended apparently by the main body of the apostles, who speedily afterwards set forth on their several journeys, to reassemble no more.

The decisions of this assembly were not less important than the occasion was interesting. After St. Peter had called attention to the first admission of a Gentile convert, and "Barnabas and Paul" had declared by what miraculous witness it had pleased God to sanction their late mission, the facts of the case were summed up by James, bishop of Jerusalem, and, according to the flesh, a near kinsman of our Lord, to whose conclusion, that nothing more should be required of Gentiles save to abstain from doing violence to Jewish feeling, the most bigoted of his countrymen for the time submitted. But in sending forth their decision, the apostles rested their authority not on arguments, which might be admitted or rejected according to the leaning of men's judgment, but on that apostolic commission, of which their miraculous powers were an apparent proof. "It seemed good to the Holy Ghost, and to us, to lay upon you no greater burden than these necessary things."[2] It is on this ground that Christians in all ages have been guided by the practice of the apostles. God was pleased to give visible attestation that they were His messengers, and therefore that the institution which they founded was accordant to His will. By virtue of this power they set apart the Lord's day for God's service instead of the seventh, or Jewish Sabbath; they taught how to observe those sacraments which Christ had ordained; they received children into the Church by baptism; they set forth the Lord's supper as the chiefest act of worship; they established two orders of ministers in the Church besides themselves: to the lowest, that of deacons, they gave the inferior service

[1] A.D. 46.   [2] Acts xv. 28.

of ministering to the poor, and assisting in the congregation: the higher order was called at first by the name either of bishops or elders—the title of elder being a Jewish name, that of bishop the Gentile appellation for those who were employed as overlookers of the people. Such ministers were placed in every city; but the rule of the Church remained altogether in the apostles themselves, or in persons whom they employed as their substitutes. Of this last number appears to have been James, the first bishop of Jerusalem, appointed probably to that office not merely from his own merit, but from reverence for his near connection with the Saviour.[1] He is often classed with the apostles, but he continued to be the settled pastor of a single city, while they separated, after the council of Jerusalem, for their various labours. The greater number travelled in Asia: some so widely, that to this day the Christians of India assert that St. Thomas visited their country, and they were at all events converted by his immediate disciples.

[1] That St. James, our Lord's kinsman, was not one of the twelve, the general, though not universal, opinion of the ancients (*vide* Burton's Lect. on Eccl. Hist. iv.) has been doubted by many later writers, because he is called an apostle, Gal. i. 19 (*vide* Tillemont, Cave, Lardner); yet the ancient opinion seems most consistent with Scripture.—1. The notion that St. James, our Lord's brother, was one of the twelve, implies him to be the son of Alphæus; and since Jude certainly was our Lord's kinsman, the same must be thought of Simon, who is twice put between them (Luke vi. 15, 16; Acts i. 13). Indeed, Lardner (vol. vi. p. 189) lays great weight on the improbability that three persons having the same names should occur both in the list of the apostles and of our Lord's brethren, and not prove to be the same persons. (This argument is overthrown by the great frequency of these names among the Jews; and, indeed, another James, another Simon, and another Jude, are found among the apostles, of whom we know for certain that they were different persons from our Lord's brethren.) Assuming, then, that James the son of Alphæus, and Simon, were both or neither of them our Lord's brethren, it is obvious that the former supposition is very inconsistent with the opposition which occurs, both before and after our Lord's death, between His apostles and His brethren: "Neither

But the labours of the great apostle of the Gentiles form the main topic of the inspired historian. On taking leave of his brethren at Jerusalem, he travelled again into Asia Minor, and thence through Macedonia into Greece. Thus was he chosen to bear witness to the faith of the cross in the chief seat of Gentile learning, and to declare in the corrupted Corinth, and the contentious Athens, that secret after which heathen philosophy had yearned in vain. Standing in the midst of Mars' hill, the seat of their chief council, the Areopagus, he preached to the Athenians that God whom they "ignorantly worshipped." Thus was the power of God's kingdom put in open opposition to the might of Satan; and some were found who received with thankfulness, from a despised Jew, what Socrates and Plato had been unable to bestow.

After testifying to our Lord's kingdom in polished Greece, St. Paul was chosen to bear the like witness at imperial Rome. He had ended his third apostolic journey by attending the feast of pentecost at Jerusalem.[1] Assaulted and accused by his brethren, he took advantage of his rights as a Roman citizen, and appealed to the emperor. The governor of Judæa sent him to the capital of the world.[2]

did His brethren believe in Him" (John vii. 5; Matt. xii. 46). And so after our Lord's crucifixion (Acts i. 14; 1 Cor. ix. 5). The same distinction may clearly be traced in eccl. hist., when the brethren of the Lord are spoken of as distinct from His apostles, Eus. iii. 11 (where Simon the son of Cleopas comes forward as a distinct man from Simon the apostle, as indeed Cave allows). Now if three of our Lord's four cousins, or half-brothers, had been among the number of the twelve, what ground could there have been for such an opposition?

2. The office of the twelve was always understood in the early Church to have been of a *missionary* kind; and the notion of fixing St. James at Jerusalem, seems to have been brought in by the Romanists, with a view of justifying them in settling St. Peter at Antioch and at Rome.

3. Those who are surprised to find St. James called an apostle after he had been appointed bishop of Jerusalem by the twelve, would probably be as unwilling to allow the same title to St. Barnabas, were it not given him in like manner, Acts xiv. 14.

[1] A.D. 53.   [2] A.D. 56.

The Roman empire was no longer under the mild and politic Augustus, whose moderation had confirmed the power which had been won by the boldness of Julius Cæsar; but Nero, the present emperor, though a monster in human shape, had not yet turned his ferocity against the Christians. St. Paul was released, after remaining two years at Rome; and he had time to visit Spain, and possibly Britain, before he returned to die as a martyr in the same city.[1]

During the latter years of St. Paul's life, he addressed letters to Timothy and Titus, two of those whom he had endowed with especial authority in the Churches which he had founded. Timothy and Titus were evidently not mere presbyters in Ephesus and Crete, where they were severally placed, because they are addressed as having the power of ordination, and an authority over those who, by right of age, would be their superiors. Yet one thing is wanting, in what can be gathered on this subject from St. Paul's epistles, and from those parts of holy Scripture which were written before or shortly after his death. We find mention, indeed, of deacons—of an order above them called either presbyters, *i.e.*, elders, or bishops, to whom the people were ordered to be obedient—and lastly, of the apostles themselves,[2] as of the "ministers of Christ, and stewards of the mysteries of God."[3] This last office had been invested with an especial character of perpetuity by our Lord's parting injunction, that they should "go, teach *all* nations;" and by His promise, to be with them "to the *end* of the world." But in what way this was to be fulfilled—whether by the miraculous preservation of their individual lives, or by the transmission of their authority to others,—required to be interpreted by the event. In what manner this system should endure, and how, as in the Jewish Church, a perpetual succession of ministers should be provided, if those were taken away who had an immediate commission from God, was not yet completely stated.

[1] A.D. 67-8.   [2] Heb. xiii. 7, 17.   [3] 1 Cor. iv. 1.

The Apostles—The Church Established.

This silence seems to have had a close connection with that which was still observed on another subject. Was the Jewish system itself to survive? As yet the apostles lived as Jews. Though St. Paul maintained that the Gentiles were free from the ceremonial law, yet he himself observed it. If the Jewish polity was to endure, the prophecies which spoke of the future greatness of God's people must apply to Israel after the flesh, not to Abraham's spiritual progeny. Did Israel and the inheritance of the tribes mean merely the possessors of the ancient promise; or was St. Paul instructed to teach some further lesson, when he called the Christian congregation the "Israel of God"? The apostles, having begun by assuming that the Church inherited the promises of the Old Testament, had confined it originally to the Jewish nation; but now that all tribes were gathered into its fold, it became necessary to prove that the promises of the Old Testament were fulfilled in the Church. Till this was established, it was uncertain what permanence would be needed for the ministers of the new covenant, and how it would fulfil those conditions which prophecy had associated with the kingdom of God.

But whatever doubts existed, they were cleared up by an event which put to trial the different systems which claimed to be God's kingdom, and decided whether the promises of old time related to temporal Israel, or to the followers of Christ. This event was the destruction of Jerusalem.[1] Our Lord had predicted it above forty years before, and St. Paul had declared it to be near at hand in his epistle to the Hebrews; at length it came, accompanied by such remarkable circumstances as shewed its great moment in the purposes of God. The Jews brought it upon themselves by their revolt against the Roman emperor Vespasian; a revolt by which they put to proof their hope that the promised kingdom of the world was to be the inheritance of their nation. "The chief motive to this

[1] A.D. 70.

unhappy war," says their own historian Josephus, "was a text which said that in those days one should come out of Judæa, who should rule the whole earth. This they applied to their own nation."[1] Vespasian, who had succeeded to the empire after the destruction of the last relics of the family of Augustus, was not less disposed to view this prediction with attention; and the surviving kinsmen of our Lord were endangered by the persecution which he exercised against the descendants of the house of David.[2]

But God left not the Jews without signs that His prophecy was to be otherwise interpreted. "What shall we say," asks Josephus, "respecting the comet that hung over Jerusalem a year together in likeness of a sword?" On the feast of pentecost, when the priests were going according to custom into the temple, they heard at first a confused murmur, and then a voice crying out in articulate words, "Let us depart hence."[3] Other signs there were, which so reminded the Christians of our Lord's prophecy, that, warned probably by the apostles, they departed to Pella, a city beyond Jordan. But by all these things the unhappy Jews were not instructed. As if the whole nation were to be taught at once that their birthright was departed, they were gathered together with one consent at Jerusalem. "A general meeting, assembled from all quarters to celebrate the passover, were engaged in the war."[4] Titus, the son of the Roman emperor, after several bloody battles, shut them up within the walls. "This vast body of people was, by the righteous providence of God, cooped up in the city as in a prison." And now, therefore, all those things fell upon them which Moses had declared to be the marks of their last rejection. That very circumstance, which before time must have seemed incredible, is declared by their own countryman to have happened.[5] "The tender

---

[1] "Wars of the Jews," vii. 12. [2] Eusebius, iii. 12.
[3] Tacitus, H'st. v. 13. [4] Josephus, vii. 16. [5] Josephus, vii. 8.

The Apostles—The Church Established. 149

and delicate woman among you, which would not adventure to set the sole of her foot upon the ground for delicateness, her eye shall be evil towards her children, which she shall bear; for she shall eat them for want of all things secretly in the siege and straitness."[1] At length the city was taken and burnt to the ground. Eleven hundred thousand of the people were killed, and a large part of the ninety-seven thousand prisoners were sent "again into Egypt," while the rest were sold for "bondsmen to their enemies."[2]

This great event, which, after a rebellion in the time of Hadrian, the Romans followed by an order that no Jew should enter Palestine,[3] was a proof to the Christians that the Jewish polity had terminated. The sceptre was now manifestly departed from them. Their captivity at Babylon had been partial and temporary. But the continued exile of the whole nation from their own land rendered the observance of Moses' law impossible. "I will shew you," says Justin Martyr, one of the earliest Christian writers, to a learned Jew, "that your sacrifice of the passover was but temporary. Here is a proof of it. God allowed the passover to be sacrificed nowhere but in the place where He put His name; foreseeing that after the suffering of Christ, this place, Jerusalem, should be given up to your enemies, and all your sacrifices come utterly to an end."[4] The same proof of the completion of the Jewish system occurs in an early collection of Christian regulations. The name and the promises which had belonged to the people of God's ancient election are there claimed as pertaining to the new. "It is impossible that in their dispersion among the Gentiles they should observe the ceremonies of the law; therefore let us Christians succeeding them inherit their promises."[5] The decision of this interesting question was forced upon the disciples of Israelitish origin by the conduct of the

---

[1] Deut. xxviii. 56-7. [2] Deut. xxviii. 68. Josephus, vii. 17.
[3] Justin, Dialog. cum Trypho, § xvi. [4] Dialog. cum Trypho, § xl.
[5] Apos. Con. vi. 25.

Romans. For when all Jews were banished from the land of their inheritance, it was only by admitting that Judaism was merged in Christianity that they could return to their ancient abode. A portion of the Jewish Christians refused to recognise this truth; and remaining at Pella, continued, as far as they could, to observe the law. But their false position threw them back after a time into the errors which they had escaped, till at length they rejected our Lord's divine character. Many, however, seem to have taken a more comprehensive view of their position, and to have discerned that because they were Christians, they were no longer Jews.[1] "Up to this time," says the historian Severus, "they united the worship of Christ with the observances of the law. But the exclusion of Jews from Jerusalem turned to the profit of the Christian faith; God so ordering it, that His Church might be freed from bondage to the Mosaic ritual."[2]

Titus is said to have believed that in destroying Jerusalem he was subverting the faith of the cross, for that Christianity must fall with Judaism, of which it was an offshoot.[3] But God rendered him an unconscious instrument in building up what he purposed to overthrow. The destruction of the parent root was essential to the vitality of its progeny. For as soon as the removal of the ancient covenant had appropriated to Christ's Church the promises of Messiah's kingdom, it became apparent that the apostles must provide whatever was needful for its permanent continuance. And this, we are told, they did. Shortly before the destruction of Jerusalem, St. James, the bishop of that parent Church,

---

[1] St. Augustine says that St. Paul observed the Mosaic law, not as necessary, but as pious and allowable for Christians of Jewish origin. Such observance, however, in his own day, he says, was no longer allowable even for them. He compares the Jewish system to a body, which, though it had "lost its life at the time of our Lord's death and resurrection," yet required honourable attendance till the time of its interment. Epist. lxxxii. 12-16.

[2] Sulp. Severus, Hist. ii. § 31.   [3] Sulp. Severus, ii. § 30.

had been murdered; and the temporary vacancy of the office, as though in anticipation of the approaching crisis, may have led the adversary to question the perpetuity of the Christian system. But no sooner had it been established by this decisive event, that the line of the apostles had superseded the line of Aaron, than "our Lord's surviving apostles and disciples met together from every quarter," to appoint the bishop who should have the guidance of the Church in Judæa.[1] And when St. John addressed the book of Revelation to the Churches of Asia a few years afterwards, a bishop, then called its angel (a name of nearly the same signification with apostle), was ruling over every single Church. Polycarp, the angel of the Church of Smyrna, afterwards a martyr for the faith, had been appointed, as we learn from his disciple Irenæus,[2] by the apostle St. John. Before the beloved apostle was taken from the earth, this order was every where established. So that the authority which St. Paul had given to Timothy and Titus is proved not to have been merely a temporary charge, coeval only with the apostle's life, but to have been a part of that office which our Lord had declared should be as abiding as the world. Hence we read in our Prayer-book,[3] that "it is manifest unto all men diligently reading holy Scripture and ancient authors, that from the apostles' time there have been these three orders in the Church,—bishops, priests, and deacons." And of this we have an especial confirmation from Ignatius, whom the apostles had appointed bishop of Antioch,[4] and who wrote letters to other Churches fifteen years only after St. John's death. Every where he speaks of the bishop as the Church's head, of priests as ordained by him to dispense the sacraments, and of deacons as their ministers. Of Christ's sacraments he speaks as he had learned from St. John, who had completed the revelation of

---

[1] Euseb. iii. 2.   [2] Irenæus, iii. 3.   A.D. 94.
[3] Preface to Ordination-service.
[4] Chrysostom, "Hom. in Ign." ii. 563.

their nature and use in his gospel, written shortly before his departure, and near seventy years after the death of our Lord. For St. John had not "tasted of death" till the consummation of the first covenant "had been fulfilled,"[1] and till the whole system of the Church had been established. Then was the last eye-witness taken away, and the testimony was bequeathed to the successors of the apostles.

---o---

APOSTOLIC MEN. THE KINGDOM OF CHRIST EXTENDED.

Difficulties of the First Successors of the Apostles—Our Lord's Presence with His Church—Unity the Sustaining Principle of His Kingdom—St. Clement—St. Ignatius—Reasons for Unity—Maintained by Community in Worship and Ordinances—Martyrdom of St. Ignatius—The Christian City—Christian Patriotism — Hegesippus — Gnostics Opposed by Testimony of Early Church—Irenæus—Great Importance of Church-System in the Infancy of Christ's Kingdom—The Church of England Appeals to its Authority—Rapid Advance of the Fifth Empire—Concord Within, and Outward Protection.

> "Then up arose a person of deep reach
>   And rare in-sight hard matters to reveal,
> That well could charm his tongue and time his speech
>   To all assaies; his name was called Zeal."—SPENSER.

IF an apostle could declare, "we have this treasure in earthen vessels," how much more deeply must the same truth have been felt by his successors! Humanly speaking, what could seem more desolate than their state? They were left in the wide world of the Roman empire to build up that spiritual kingdom by which it was to be suc-

[1] A.D. 100.

ceeded. Its strength and greatness, the injustice of its officers, the cruelty of its princes, the contempt of the learned, the violence of the people,—how were these to be resisted by that handful of poor, untaught, unarmed "strangers who were scattered over"[1] its vast dominions? And now that the apostles were gone, miracles either ceased, or were wrought seldom and by few. What means were there for building up this fifth kingdom, which could be compared with the wealth of Nebuchadnezzar, the virtue of Cyrus, the enterprise of Alexander, or the fortune of Rome?

The absence of other miracles exhibits with greater clearness that grand and lasting wonder, *the Saviour's presence in His Church from age to age.* By His Spirit He was with it; so that it neither lacked wisdom nor zeal; so that the apostolic men, to whom His kingdom had been entrusted, moved on resistless in the way of His will. "We have this treasure in earthen vessels, that the excellency of the power may be of God, and not of us." And the two great types, which had been given of old time, shewed them whither their efforts were conducting—the history of God's ancient people, which had been the spiritual preparation for the kingdom of Christ; and that of those four earthly empires, which had been its temporal forerunners. To each of these had the Church been likened in holy Scripture. It was the new Jerusalem, and therefore it must have the distinguishing privilege of ancient Israel, one common worship: it was the fifth kingdom, and therefore, like the four preceding, it must have one common government. And such was the fabric which the Spirit of God raised up, notwithstanding every obstacle. For so scattered as were the early Christians, composed of many nations, using different languages, with different laws, habits, and prejudices, with no central place, like Jerusalem, where they should meet for worship, nor any single earthly potentate, like the Roman emperor, to whom they should owe obedience,—how unlikely were

[1] 1 Pet. i. 1.

they to maintain one united worship or one common government! There could be no earthly centre for common worship, when the city was gone which had been hallowed by the Lord's presence; and as yet the Roman bishop had not made the least show of pretending to that tyrannous power which he afterwards usurped. The wide dispersion of the Christians is thus strikingly described by one of their number,[1] in this first generation which followed the apostles: "The Christians are distinguished neither in country, speech, nor government from other men. They neither dwell in towns of their own, use their own dialect, nor any peculiar mode of life. . . . They occupy Greek or barbarian cities, as their lot may be; but following their country's rule in dress and manners, they propose to themselves the establishment of what is doubtless a strange and marvellous institution. . . . They inhabit their native country, yet as sojourners. With the privileges of citizens they submit to the condition of strangers. Every foreign land becomes their country, yet every country is foreign. . . . For they dwell upon earth, but their citizenship is in heaven. . . . They obey the appointed laws, yet outrun them by their individual excellence. In a word, what the soul is to the body, such to the world are the Christians. As all the body's members are animated by the soul, so are the Christians scattered through all cities of the earth."

In such a wide-spread body we might well expect to find no agreement, but that the same name would be associated with every various form of worship and government: but where then would have been the new Jerusalem, which was to exhibit its one collective worship, and where that fifth kingdom, which was to be one government like the preceding four? Now our Lord had predicted that His people should be one, not in name only, but, as He Himself was one with the Father, in truth;[2] and in His wisdom He so constituted His Church, that it remained one, both in

[1] Ep. ad Diogn. "apostolorum discipulus," § 5. [2] John xvii. 21.

inward worship and in outward form. This followed from the manner in which its blessings were given. His disciples taught that its advantages were not bestowed on men except as members of that one great community, which they were every where ordered to extend. There was no such thing as being a Christian apart. That gift of God's grace, which was implanted in the heart of every sincere believer as the "earnest" of heavenly blessedness, had its abode in the midst of the Church, and diffused itself severally to all its members. Only, therefore, in the Christian community was there the presence of the Holy Ghost. The Church was a hallowed soil, which was every where forming itself amidst the treacherous quicksands of heathen ignorance. To worship with it, was to draw near to the fountain of grace; to partake in its sacraments worthily, was to obtain the Holy Spirit. We read of but one place where these truths met with opposition,—the wealthy and luxurious city of Corinth. Even during St. Paul's lifetime, he had found it needful to reprove its inhabitants for their divisions; and shortly after his death there arose new troubles, because "one or two persons rebelled against the ministers" to whose charge they had been committed.[1] Several of the apostles were still living; but as St. Peter and St. Paul, the chief of those who had travelled into the west, were removed,[2] the Church at Corinth applied for advice to St. Clement, who was then bishop of Rome. St. Clement's reply remains —one of the most interesting documents in Church-history, both because it shews that the Church of Rome at that time asserted no claim to govern other Christian societies, and also because it discovers the state of feeling about the time[3] of the destruction of Jerusalem, before the already ascertained offices of bishop and priest had been discriminated by the names which afterwards distinguished them.

St. Clement, like St. Paul, speaks much of the necessity of union, and of the unchristian nature of religious divisions.

[1] St. Clem. i. § 47.   [2] St. Clem. i. § 5.   [3] A.D. 70.

"Have we not one God, and one Christ, and one Spirit of grace which has been poured out upon us, and one calling in Christ? . . . why do we oppose ourselves to the body of which we are ourselves a part, and forget that we are members one of another?"[1] He reminds the Corinthians, that since our Lord had, through His apostles, appointed a peculiar order in His Church, unity and peace could be procured in no other way than by submission. "We ought to do every thing which the Lord ordained in its appointed way. He ordered that our sacramental offerings and our public prayers should not be performed rashly and at random, but in their prescribed season and time. And *where* He would have them performed, and through the agency of *what persons*, He has Himself decided by His sovereign will. That all things being duly performed and to His good pleasure, may be acceptable before Him. Those, therefore, who render their sacramental services in the appointed manner are accepted and happy. By obeying the Master's injunctions, they are free from error. For the chief priest has his peculiar ministrations committed to him; the priests have their own place assigned them; the Levites are bound to their appropriate duties; the laity is bound to lay services.

"Let each one of you, my brethren, remaining conscientiously in his own station, render thanks to God, not overstepping the appointed rule of his service, in all honour." Then, after touching upon the exact obedience which was required under the Jewish law, he contrasts it with the still more loyal reverence which might be expected from those who lived under the "law of liberty." "To them, if doing ought contrary to what His will prescribed, death is assigned as the punishment. Consider, brethren, whether, as we have been thought worthy of greater knowledge, we are not exposed to a heavier penalty. To us the apostles have delivered the Gospel from Jesus Christ our Lord.

[1] St. Clem. § 46.

Christ was sent from God, the apostles from Christ. So far, then, the will of God was exactly followed. The apostles having received their charge, having been confirmed by the resurrection of Jesus Christ, and strengthened by the full assurance of the Holy Ghost, went forth to declare the coming of the kingdom of God. When preaching in every country and city, they appointed the first-fruits of their disciples, having made trial of them by the Holy Ghost, to be bishops and curates[1] for them that believe. The apostles knew, by our Lord's teaching, that strife would arise concerning the bishop's office; and therefore, having perfect knowledge of what would happen, they appointed those of whom I have spoken, and gave a succession for time to come, that when they fell asleep, other approved men might inherit their ministry."[2]

Such is the view given of Christ's Church during the lifetime of the apostles, by one of whom holy Scripture witnesses that his "name was in the book of life."[3] But, it may be said, could not God's grace be bestowed otherwise? Can we limit His power to one single channel? Was not the WORD present with the patriarchs of old? May not God have continued to bestow His grace more widely? This inquiry is foreign to the present narrative. The question is not, what *may* be the extent of God's mercies; but by what means it pleased Him to raise up that fabric of the Church which He "built upon the foundation of the apostles, Jesus Christ Himself being the chief corner-stone." This can only be gathered from what was actually done by the apostles, and by those holy men whom they employed as their chief instruments. The words of one such, St. Clement, have been given, and they

---

[1] Literally "bishops and deacons." It has been stated that at this time, A.D. 70, the names of the three offices were not exactly discriminated, though the offices themselves were so. This seems best expressed by taking an expression which our Church has employed with the same latitude.

[2] St. Clement, i. § 40-44. [3] Phil. iv. 3.

shew the judgment of the whole Christian community; for, as being universally approved, they were long wont to be read in public worship for the instruction of the whole congregation. No less regard was felt for the sayings of another martyr of that age, Ignatius, concerning whom the Church of Antioch testifies that his letters "abound with the spirit of grace, in prayer and exhortation."

His six epistles to the chief Churches of that day,[1] not only exhibit his faith and piety in the near prospect of being taken to Him whom not seeing "he loved," but they shew likewise what course God's providence was taking for building up the kingdom of Christ. Ignatius had been appointed bishop of Antioch in the latter days of St. John, and when the different members which make up the body of Christ had been distinguished in name as well as in office. He speaks often, and in their several order, of bishops, priests, and deacons. "Where these orders," he says, "are not found, there can be no Church."[2] "Let no one take any part in Church offices without the bishop's sanction. Let that be esteemed to be a real celebration of the Lord's supper which is performed by the bishop, or by some one whom he appoints. Where they have the bishop's guidance, there let the congregation attend; just as where Christ Jesus is, there is the Catholic Church. Without the bishop's authority, it is neither lawful to baptise nor to celebrate the communion."[3]

This close attention to the Church's order Ignatius does not state merely as a positive command, though that were reason enough for obedience; but he speaks of it as the means of procuring those gifts of grace which are the peculiar privilege of Christians. These gifts are obtained only by union with Christ. Men cannot be united to Christ except by being members of the Church, which is His body. "Let no one," he says, "be deceived. Unless a man comes to the Church's altars, he is deprived of the

[1] A.D. 107. [2] Trallians, § 3. [3] Smyrnæans, § 8.

bread of life. For if the prayer of one or two is of such avail, how much more that of the bishops and of the collective Church!"[1] "If any follows a divider, he will not have his lot in the kingdom of God. Be careful, therefore, to join in the one eucharist. For the flesh of our Lord Jesus Christ is but one, and one cup only is there whereby we participate in His blood. There is one altar, one bishop, with the priests and deacons, my fellow-servants."[2]

This constant mention of the ordinances and ministers of the Church is attended by perpetual reference to the gifts of grace, as rendering them so important. Christians are to remember to be in communion with the bishops, "that they may be one, not in form merely, but in spirit."[3] For to the collective body of bishops, as representatives of the whole Church, Ignatius looked, as inheriting that gift of our Lord's presence which had so solemnly been bestowed upon the college of apostles. "The bishops, who have been appointed throughout the whole extent of the world, make up the mind of Christ."[4] And this principle, that the several public officers of all the Churches made up that united body of Christ with which He was ever present—a principle to which Ignatius pledged himself in the immediate prospect of death—"with those who reverence their bishops, priests, and deacons, may my lot be in God!"[5] —the Christian community maintained for many years by constant intercourse among its different portions. Tertullian writes[6] nearly one hundred years later, "the many and numerous Churches which now exist make up that original one which was founded by the apostles. Thus all are primitive and all apostolic, while all prove themselves to be the same community: for they are bound together by a common affection; they bestow upon one another the name of brethren; and they exchange the rights of friendship.'

[1] Ephesians, § 5. [2] Philadelphians, § 3. [3] Magnesians, § 13.
[4] Ephes. § 3. [5] To Polycarp, § 6. [6] De Præscrip. § 20.

This intercourse was maintained by means of commendatory letters from the several bishops, which entitled any member of their Churches who travelled abroad to be received into the communion of any other Christian society. When bishops themselves visited foreign cities, the unity of their commission was recognised by their sharing in the celebration of the holy communion. Thus, when Polycarp, bishop of Smyrna, visited Rome, in the time of Anicetus,[1] he bore the chief part in the consecration of the sacred elements, as a token that his character as a brother bishop was admitted by the Bishop of Rome. Thus was St. Paul's saying fulfilled, that "if one member suffered, all the members suffered with it; and if one member rejoiced, all the members rejoiced with it." When the same Polycarp offered himself as a confessor for the faith of Christ, the Church over which he had ruled sent the news of his warfare in the common cause "to all the dioceses of the Catholic Church." The circumstances of Ignatius's own martyrdom[2] were in like manner widely circulated, and have been handed down to our time. They are rendered memorable not only by his high office and character—a favourite disciple of St. John, appointed to rule over the Church where the name of Christians had first arisen—but also because in him the kingdom of Christ came into contact with one of the chiefest champions of that fourth empire, which it was destined to survive.

In the ninth year of his reign, the Emperor Trajan, elated with his victory over the Scythians, Dacians, and many other nations, and thinking that, to complete his conquest, nothing remained but to overthrow the impious system of the Christians, threatened to persecute those who would not join in that dæmon-worship which all mankind approved, and compelled the saints either to sacrifice or die. Then was this noble soldier of Christ (Ignatius) alarmed for the Church of Antioch, and he presented him-

---

[1] A.D. 158.   [2] A.D. 107. Martyrium S. Ignatii.

self to Trajan, who was at that time in the place, and full of his plans of marching into Armenia against the Parthians. He stood face to face with the emperor, when this dialogue arose :—

Trajan. "Wretch! what evil spirit possesses you, that you are a daring transgressor of my commands, and lead on others to their ruin?"

Ignatius. "He with whom God abides is possessed by no spirit of evil, for the evil spirits have departed from the servants of God."

Trajan. "With whom does God abide?"

Ignatius. "With him who has Christ in his bosom."

Trajan. "And think you not that my soul too is inhabited by gods, since I use them as my assistants against my enemies?"

Ignatius. "You err in calling those spirits gods whom the heathen worship; for there is one God, who made heaven and earth, the sea and all that is therein; and one Jesus Christ, the only begotten Son of God, in whose kingdom may I have my portion!"

Trajan. "Do you speak of Him who was crucified in the time of Pontius Pilate?"

Ignatius. "I speak of Him who crucified my sin with its author; and who trod all devilish deceit and crime under the feet of them in whose hearts he inhabits."

Trajan. "Do you, then, bear this crucified one within you?"

Ignatius. "Yes; for it is written, I will dwell in them, and walk in them."

Trajan. "We enjoin that Ignatius, who says that he bears the crucified within him, should be carried by soldiers to the mighty city of Rome, there to be the food of wild beasts, as a spectacle to the people."

And thus they parted—the one to triumph over the utmost East, the other to die amidst the derision of the capital of the West. Thus did the might of the flesh gain a momentary victory over the might of the spirit; for who could gainsay the emperor's will? Instantly was Ignatius seized by ten soldiers, almost as savage as the monsters who were to devour him, and dragged through vast regions and over wide seas, till he was cast to wild beasts in the very heart of that great empire whose power he had resisted. He had stood up a solitary man against the matchless strength of that iron kingdom. "How easily was he trampled to the earth, as by some resistless engine rushing forward and crushing all that opposed it! So it went on its way, that proud and mighty empire, wearing away the saints of the Most High. But its hour came; it crumbled, and passed away. Its palaces are dust; its provinces have passed from one conqueror to another; its populous capital is slowly sinking into desolation; its very memory has faded from the lands wherein it ruled. 'So let all Thine enemies perish, O Lord!'"[1]

Ignatius suffered martyrdom only about seven years after the death of the beloved apostle; but his friend Polycarp was spared above fifty years longer as a witness to the truth. He had been appointed bishop by St. John; and his continuance in that conspicuous post during half the second century affords one of those connecting links by which the system of the apostles was perpetuated. At length, in the reign of Antoninus,[2] we read of his appearance before the Roman governor of proconsular Asia. "'Respect your age,' said the Roman; 'swear by the fortune of Cæsar; repent, and say, Take away the atheists.' Polycarp, waving his hand, with a melancholy glance towards the multitude, said, as he looked up with a sigh to heaven, 'Take away the atheists.' The governor continued to urge him: 'Take the oath, and I will release you: revile Christ.' 'Eighty and six years,' replied Polycarp, 'have I been his servant, and he has never injured me; how, then, can I revile my Saviour and my King?' Being still further importuned to

---

[1] Sermon by the Rev. H. W. Wilberforce on the rebuilding of St. Lawrence's Church, Southampton.   [2] A.D. 167.

swear by the fortune of Cæsar, he said, 'If you think it possible that I can comply, and pretend to be ignorant of my character, hear at once who I am, *my name is Christian.*'"

Wheresoever the masters of the world turned, they found, in like manner, that their power was limited; and that the fifth kingdom, which was growing up among them, possessed a dominion over the hearts of its subjects which could not be done away. Ten years after the martyrdom of Polycarp we have a similar witness in the West to the absorbing interest which it had gained over the minds of men. The Churches of Lyons and Vienne, in Gaul, were at that time enduring a fierce persecution, in which Pothinus, bishop of Lyons, was martyred. At this time we are told that a Christian named Sanctus was tortured with peculiar cruelty, his enemies expecting that the intensity of his sufferings "would force from him some unbecoming reply. But so great was his constancy, that, in answer to all their demands, he would neither mention his own name, nor the name of his city, nor his country, nor whether he were bond or free; but, in reply to every demand, he said, 'I am a Christian.' This one thing comprised his name, city, country, and condition." [1]

The feeling and principle which attached so much importance to the very name of Christian, is illustrated at a somewhat later period in the history of certain Egyptian martyrs. Firmilian, the Roman officer before whom they were brought, asked the name of one whom by many tortures he had been unable to induce to sacrifice. "Instead of his own name, the martyr returned one taken from the prophets; for he and his companions had renounced the idolatrous names which had been given them, and had joined themselves to God's true Israel, not only in act, but in their very appellations. The governor, not able to understand the name he gave, asked next what was his

[1] Euseb. v. 1.

country. He replied in like manner, that his country was Jerusalem, referring to St. Paul's words, 'Jerusalem from above is the mother of us all;' and, again, 'we are come to the city of the living God, the heavenly Jerusalem.' To this city were his thoughts turning. But Firmilian, fixed upon what was present, was debating in his mind what city, and where this might be. With further tortures he sought to extort a true confession, and asked often what city was this, and in what country did it lie. 'It is the city which belongs exclusively to God's servants. No others can partake in it. It may be seen in the utmost east, even under the rising sun.' Thus did the martyr pursue his own train of thought, regardless of the violence of his persecutors. But the governor was agitated and confused, supposing that the Christians were surely designing to found some city which should be hostile to the Roman name."[1]

And a city the Christians were truly building—that one Church Catholic, which had everywhere one name and one communion, because one Jesus Christ was everywhere present with it all. This truth Irenæus witnesses, who, having in early youth been Polycarp's disciple, was presbyter of the Church in Gaul during the persecution of Antoninus,[2] and was made bishop of Lyons after the martyrdom of Pothinus. Polycarp had lived during the first half of that century which followed St. John's death; Irenæus teaches us the Church's doings during its second portion. He declares what faith the Christians "had received from the apostles and their disciples." And this faith, he says, "the Church, though scattered throughout the whole world, guards diligently, as though it inhabited a single mansion. It has the same faith, because it has but one heart and one soul; and because it has but one mouth, it teaches and delivers the same accordant words: and though different languages prevail in different countries, yet one sense only is inculcated. In no place is there any private creed or

[1] Eus. de Marty. Palæst. § 11.　　　　[2] A.D. 177.

peculiar opinion; not in Germany nor in Spain; not among the Gauls or in the East; not in Egypt, Lybia, or the central parts of the civilised world;—but, as God's creature, the sun, stands singly forth, and is equally visible throughout the earth, in like manner is the preaching of the truth manifested; and it, too, gives light to every one that cometh into the world." [1]

It was surely a wonderful sight, when men were so daring as thus to cast away their lives for a name, and yet bowed so submissively to the yoke of apostolic doctrine. No common principle could possess the propagators of the Christian system. What their principle was, cannot be doubted by those who believe that the Lord of life is truly present with His Church; and that whenever it goes forth in His name, with zeal, meekness, and purity, no power in earth or hell can prevail for its defeat. Christ's dwelling with His whole Church is the secret of the establishment of His kingdom. His servants fought with an unconquerable belief that He was ever near: but that their belief was not only confident but lasting, that it filled not only ardent but profound minds, arose from this one circumstance, that He was with them in truth. His presence was not a fiction, but a fact. This it was which allayed the tortures of the martyr, which gave energy to the thoughtful spirit, and quickened the whole body of the Church. And it pleased Him who can make the simplest means His instrument, to render this oneness of spirit, which the Church drew necessarily from its common Head, the most powerful agent in its growth and vigour. All Christians were one, because through one outward instrument, the Church, they participated in our Lord's spiritual presence; and this unity preserved the simplicity of their faith, and animated their labours of love. The writings of the early Christians are distinguished by a noble self-forgetfulness, which saw all in Christ, which sought all through the advancement of His kingdom, which knew no

[1] Iren. i. 10, § 2.

private interest; so that men could scarce find room to speak of their own feelings, in their anxiety for the welfare of the universal Church. And this Christian patriotism had its reward. Their enlarged affections redounded to their individual benefit. They gave their labour to the establishment of Christ's kingdom, and He engrafted them into His mystic body; they were anxious that His power should be exalted, and He made their sons to grow up as young plants, and their daughters to be as the polished corners of the temple.

This feeling of the unity of the Church was the predominating idea of the early Christians. They describe it as one mighty town,[1] compacted together by the union of individual Christians; or as one great nation,[2] inheriting the name and promises of ancient Israel. They looked at it as one, not in name only, but in life; as the one body of Christ, as the one kingdom which was to prevail among the nations. Its establishment they perceived to be the greatest event in the history of the world; its blessings the chiefest of which the children of men could be partakers. Hence when Hegesippus would write a sequel to the Acts of the Apostles, he first visited every Church from Palestine to Italy, that he might be assured of the perfect unity of that vast body which then bore the name of Christian. This remarkable inquiry was made fifty years after St. John's death;[3] and we learn the result of his observations from those who wrote when his history (now lost) was in the hands of all men. "As yet," he says, "the Church retains its original purity; everywhere I have conversed with the bishops, and have found that in every city, and in every successive appointment of their predecessors, the Church's laws have been observed. I have received from all of them the same statement of their doctrines." When Hegesippus made this inquiry, the first generation of bishops was not

---

[1] Hermas's Pastor. [2] Apos. Con. ubi sup.
[3] A.D. 150. Eusebius, iv. 22.

yet extinct: and the apostles had been directed to the wisest means of attaining this concord; for they had appointed "the first-fruits of their disciples" to this important office.[1] The testimony of such men served to decide any doubts which might arise as to the doctrines of the Gospel.

Of this we have an instance towards the end of the second century, when certain persons proposed to give a different view of the truth of God from that which had always been received in the Churches. They were called Gnostics, because they thought that by their own knowledge (*gnosis*) they could understand the apostles better than the Christian teachers of their day, and could enter further into the words of Christ than the very apostles who transmitted them. Against these innovators Irenæus wrote,[2] and somewhat later Tertullian.[3] And they appeal always to the consistent testimony of those bishops and Churches that lived in communion together throughout the world. "Whatever secret mysteries the apostles had known," says Irenæus,[4] "they would naturally have imparted them most fully to those to whom they committed the care of the Churches." "We can number up those who have been appointed bishops in the several Churches by the apostles, and mention their successors to this very hour." "Let *these* men," says Tertullian,[5] "declare the origin of their Churches; let them unroll the order of their bishops; let them shew it to have commenced from the beginning; so that each bishop had an apostle, or apostolic man, as the original sanction of his succession. For in this way it is that the apostolic Churches produce their pedigree: thus does Rome refer to Clement, who was consecrated by St. Peter; and Smyrna to Polycarp, who was appointed by St. John."

As an individual instance of this powerful appeal, take

---

[1] St. Clement's Epistle, ubi sup.
[2] A.D. 120 to A.D. 202.
[3] A.D. 150 to A.D. 220.
[4] Iren. iii. 3, § 1.
[5] De Præscrip. § 32.

the letter of Irenæus to Florinus, who had been seduced into the Gnostic heresy. "These, Florinus, to use a mild expression, are no wholesome doctrines. They are not accordant with the teaching of the Church; they lead to the greatest impiety. . . . It was not thus that we were taught by the elders who had enjoyed converse with the apostles. I remember as a boy to have seen you with Polycarp in Lower Asia; you, with good prospects in the emperor's court, wished, however, to secure his approbation. What happened then I remember better than recent occurrences. For the instruction which we receive in childhood, growing with our growth, becomes identified with ourselves. So that I can remember the place where the blessed Polycarp sat and talked—his coming in and going out—the character of his life—his outward form—his sermons to the people—his account of his intercourse with St. John, and the others who had seen the Lord—and what he stated concerning their words, and the account they had given him respecting the Lord. And Polycarp's statement respecting our Lord's miracles and teaching, derived from eye-witnesses of the word of life, is in exact accordance with the Scriptures. All this, by God's mercy, I then listened to with interest, storing it up, not in books, but in the table of my heart."[1]

These extracts suggest cause for thankfulness to God's mercy, in that He was pleased to build His Church upon the foundation of the apostles and prophets. The written word, the rule of Christian belief, might have been all that was vouchsafed to us. The new Testament might have been given at once, without aught to guide men into its system and signification. God was pleased to deal otherwise. He was pleased to secure the right interpretation of His word in that first age, when it was most important, by establishing the system of His Church before the Scriptures were in the hands of Christians. When Clement wrote to

[1] Eusebius, v. 20.

the Corinthians, three gospels only were in being, yet the WORD was worshipped in the western Church; and our Lord's body and blood were known to be spiritually present in the holy communion, as certainly as after those truths had been more clearly revealed in St. John's gospel. When Pantænus, in the middle of this century, went as a missionary to India,[1] he found Christians there, in union with the universal Church, yet acquainted with no part of Scripture but St. Matthew's gospel. Of other disciples we hear, even at a later period, that they had no written Scriptures at all. But they had "the apostles' doctrine," that "gospel" which St. Paul had "received," "the form of sound words" in which Timothy continued.[2]

We thank God, therefore, not only for the gift of the Scriptures, but also for that institution of His Church which was in being before the Scriptures were written, and without which they would not have produced that unity of belief which led to the speedy growth of Christ's kingdom. For had the Scriptures been given, as a naked depository of new facts, into the hands of men, each one would have judged of them by himself; the appeal would have been rather to the head than the heart, and private study would have been more esteemed than that gift of grace which God bestows. Hence faith would have flourished less than reasoning. Every one would have had his own view of truth, until truth had seemed to be with no one. This was actually the case with those bold men, who, in the first century after the apostles' time, laid their hands upon holy writ, and undertook by their own wit to explain it. Their arguments on Scripture, whether with one another or with Christians, had no end. It was easy, indeed, to confute, but it was impossible to silence. "It is useless," says Tertullian,[3] "to appeal in such cases to Scripture; for when no victory can be gained, or none but what is doubtful, you ought not to enter into dispute. True, you will lose nothing but your

---

[1] Eusebius, v. 10. [2] Acts xi. 42; 1 Cor. xv. 12; 2 Tim. i. 13.
[3] De Præscrip, § 17, 19

breath in the contest; but then you will gain nothing but indignation at your opponents' blasphemy."

How different had been the Church's progress in that tender state, if there had been no means by which such dangers could be averted! If her trunk had been split and her roots dissevered, how could she have become the greatest among the trees of the forest? How could the weak be expected to hazard their lives, if even the strong had no assurance what were the true doctrines of the apostles? How many would have rejected a system on which its advocates could not agree! While each man was building up his own system, the magnificent prospects of Christ's kingdom would have been lost amidst the diversity of opinions. If this spectacle is so injurious even to the established age of the Christian Church, how fatal had it been at its commencement! But this danger it pleased God to obviate. And what prevented it was, that His will was not only conveyed in a book, on which the proud and captious could employ their reason, but embodied, likewise, in that system to which the meek and humble surrendered their hearts. Thus, by the teaching of apostolic men were they guided into the meaning of the apostles. "When there are such clear modes of proof," says Irenæus,[1] "we ought not to seek elsewhere for that certainty which the Church readily supplies, inasmuch as to it, as to an abundant storehouse, the apostles committed an ample supply of truth." This was the confidence which sustained the disciple of Polycarp among the barbarous Gauls to whom he witnessed. A few years later another voice replies from a different continent: "Would you have some further assurance respecting the doctrines of salvation? Run through the apostolical Churches, still ruled by authorities established by the apostles themselves, where their authentic letters are read, and which seem, therefore, to utter their voice and to retain their presence. Are you near Achaia?

[1] Irenæus, iii. 4, § 1.

you can have recourse to Corinth. Do you border on Macedonia? look at Thessalonica and Philippi. If you can cross into Asia, you have Ephesus. Are you near Italy? there is Rome."[1]

This was a decisive method of determining the meaning of Scripture, because there was no question what system was taught by these various Churches. And on this account it is that the Church of England has declared that the right meaning of holy Scripture, the real mind of God's Spirit, is that form of belief which was promulgated by those apostolical men whom our Lord employed to build up His kingdom. Her ministers are enjoined[2] not to teach any thing as the meaning of Scripture except that view of truth which had the consentient approbation of the ancient fathers: and even her laity are required to join in their declarations of essential doctrine; for from them comes the creed which the Church requires every man to receive who is admitted into her communion. And this she requires, because so much as this was thought needful in that first age by those who had received instruction from the apostles; for since Christ's kingdom was to consist of men bound together by that communion with the Church's Head which required that they should receive Him as their Saviour, it was needful that they should make some profession of their faith when they were admitted into the ranks of them that believed. And this confession,[3] whether commanded by

[1] Tertullian. de Præs., § xxxvi.

[2] "Preachers shall see that they teach nothing in the congregation as to be religiously received and believed by the people, except what is accordant to the doctrine of the Old and New Testament, and what has been collected from that doctrine by the Catholic fathers and ancient bishops."—"Canons," 1571. Wilkins' "Concilia," iv. 267.

[3] The manner of making this confession we have from the story of Victorinus, as recorded by St Augustine :—

"When the hour was come for making profession of his faith, which at Rome they, who are about to approach to Thy grace, deliver, from an elevated place, in the sight of all the faithful, in a set form of words committed to memory, the presbyters, he said, offered Victhe apostles, or appointed by those who followed in the first age, contained a declaration of belief in the three persons of the Godhead, in whose names they were to be baptised—in the reality of the Church, that kingdom of Christ which they desired to join—and of their confidence that the forgiveness of sins and a future hope might be obtained by the Christian covenant. These fundamental truths, which, under the name of the Apostles' Creed, our Church requires all worshippers to acknowledge, have been delivered down to us from the time when all who confessed them joined in one communion, and made up one spiritual kingdom.

And how goodly was its advance! Pass a hundred years from the time when the last apostle was taken away, and already the Church began to rise above the crumbling ruins of that empire which it was shortly to succeed. "We are but of yesterday," exclaimed the Christians, "and we have filled your whole realm,—your cities, islands, fortresses, municipalities—your councils, your very camps, your assemblies, your forum, — no where but in your temples are you alone."[1]

---

torinus, as was customary in the case of such as seemed likely through bashfulness to be alarmed, to make his profession more privately: but he chose rather to profess his salvation in the presence of the holy multitude. 'For it was not salvation that he taught in rhetoric, and yet that he publicly professed: how much less then ought he, when pronouncing Thy word, to dread Thy meek flock, who, when delivering his own words, had not feared multitudes of madmen.' When, then, he went up to make his profession, all, as they knew him, uttered his name, one to another, with a cry of congratulation. And who there knew him not? and a hushed sound ran through the lips of the rejoicing assembly, Victorinus! Victorinus! Sudden was the sound of exultation that they saw him; sudden also the silence of attention, that they might hear him. He pronounced the true faith with an excellent boldness, and all wished to draw him into their very heart," &c.—"St Augustine's Confessions," book viii. [Chapter ii. page 138 in the edition of this series.—ED.]

[1] Tert. Apol. § xxxvii.

Such were the effects of Christ's presence with His Church in the day of its inward unity. This first century after the removal of the apostles, which was measured out by the successive lives of Polycarp [1] and Irenæus,[2] was its season of youth. Ignorance and corruption must have existed in a community surrounded by heathen darkness, and itself newly born out of the night of paganism; yet there was a docility which accustomed men to walk quietly in the path which God had appointed, and an unwavering assurance that the path was not mistaken. For as yet there was no doubt what was Christ's kingdom, and how men were to enter into communion with His mystic body. No Christian could doubt the authority of those whom the apostles had made rulers of the Churches, nor deny that holy Scripture was rightly understood by those who had apostolic men for their instructors. Each man used his judgment to learn that system which was delivered, and not to discover for himself that system which would be best; and therefore it was not difficult to agree. Men came to the Church not as objectors, but as disciples; they learnt not by criticism, but by testimony,—not by reasoning respecting doctrines, but by inquiry respecting facts.

And in this course the Church was much benefited by that very greatness of the Roman empire, which might at first sight threaten to impede it. The internal peace which it produced among the various nations of the world, the opportunities of intercourse which it afforded, contributed to maintain that unity of the faith which so greatly tended towards the growth of Christ's kingdom. As God's people of old time grew and multiplied under the shelter of Egyptian civilisation, so this fourth persecuting empire did but foster the seed which it sought to extirpate. Prudentius, a Christian poet of the fifth century, assigns this as the reason why that worldly kingdom should have been allowed to grow to such gigantic greatness:

[1] A.D. 68 to 167.   [2] A.D. 120 to 202.

> " For say, O Roman, why thy stern behest
> Sways the wi le regions of the east and west;
> Why nations in their tongue and faith diverse
> Bow to thy will, thy laws and speech rehearse:
> One city only and one people spread
> From Tagus' flood to far Himalas' head; [1]
> Why, but to hush the jarring sounds of war,
> And smooth the pathway for Messiah's car,
> That numerous tribes, by laws and arts combined,
> Might to the cross submit their captive mind." [2]

———o———

EARLY SCHISMATICS. MONTANUS AND NOVATIAN.

Principle of Schism—Montanus—Tertullian—Novatian—State of Christians during the Decian Persecution—Puritans—Pacian—Christ's Kingdom Re-United.

> " Ne let vain words bewitch thy manly heart,
> Ne devilish thoughts dismay thy constant spright;
> In heavenly mercies hast not thou a part?
> Why shouldst thou then despair, that chosen art?
> Where justice grows, there grows eke greater grace,
> The which doth quench the brand of hellish smart,
> And that accurs'd handwriting doth deface."—SPENSER.

SUCH was the victory of Christ's Church in the century which followed the death of the apostles. Error and ignorance were indeed found in it, because ignorant and erring men were continually entering its ranks; but these evils took no hold upon it,—they were continually purged off as foreign to its nature, and inconsistent with its transmitted principles of truth. But, besides these outward evils, there arose divisions which had their root in the Church's

---

[1] When Prudentius speaks of those whom "Ganges alit," he must have referred rather to the influence than the empire of Rome.

[2] Adapted from Prudentius in Sym. ii. § 5.

inner nature, and therefore must appear from time to time, so long as she continues in this militant state. For heresy, however fatal, is an outward and temporary disorder; but schism, however trivial, is an inward and lasting ill.

In modern times schism has often been but one form of insubordination, and has been frequently wedded to that political feeling which discerns that the best engine against governments is to destroy the religion which sustains them. But such was not the nature or object of schism in ancient days. It arose before the Christian faith had found favour with senates and rulers, and had a deeper and purer root. For since Christians are united not merely, like the dwellers in one land, by a territorial limit, but also by their allegiance to a common faith, they are liable to differences, according as some men forget the common principle which they profess, and others carry it to an unnatural extent. Even before the persecutions under the Emperor Antoninus,[1] in which Polycarp and Pothinus had suffered, the principles of the cross had been forgotten by many who professed the faith of the Crucified, and the kingdom of Christ contained citizens whose lives shewed that they were not obedient subjects. Thence arose the wish for some stricter bond, for some more certain principle of union, which might constrain the obedient and exclude the careless. A body less extensive than the body of Christ—a society less numerous than that which He feeds with sacraments and has bought with His blood—a kingdom more concentrated than His universal empire—a Church within a Church, less promiscuous than that merciful home, the asylum of the weak, the timid, and the penitent;—this has, in all ages, been the wish of earnest and ardent Christians, except when guided by an unchangeable faith, or tempered by an overpowering humility, or when a large insight into life has extended the sphere of their observation.

Such was the temper of the first dissenters,—the enthu-

[1] A.D. 167 and 177.

siastic Montanus and the austere Novatian. They were schismatics, not heretics; for they were seditious members, not open enemies of Christ's kingdom,—they rebelled against the Church, without abandoning her creed: not that even they cast off the authority of bishops,[1] nor denied the necessity of sacraments; for these things during fifteen centuries after Christ were never called in question by any who professed themselves Christians.

The first of these separatists, Montanus, who arose about seventy years after St. John's death,[2] thought himself guided by the especial influence of that Spirit which our Lord had promised to His disciples. The presence of the Comforter was not, he said, a general indwelling in the Church at large, but its peculiar abode in such favoured persons as himself. In dependence on this conviction, he presumed to give laws to those who gathered round him in his native Phrygia. Many believed him to possess really the power of prophecy. His most celebrated follower was Tertullian; the most eloquent of the Latin fathers, a man of stern and self-denying temper, whose able writings in defence of the Gospel did not prevent him, any more than our own countryman Law, from being beguiled in his later years by the visions of an inferior understanding. Thus have the greatest minds been not unfrequently a prey to the delusions of mysticism. One reason is, that in the depths of our mental constitution there are dark and mysterious secrets, over which superficial observers glide with a contented and incurious facility, but which men of searching intellects can slightly discern, but cannot penetrate. Such weakness casts a stronger light upon that law of our moral nature, which makes humility the necessary condition for discovering truth.

Thus did there arise a faction within the kingdom of Christ, during the first century after the days of the apostles, which claimed to itself to be the sole guardian of the creed, and to be the inheritor of the Church's name and promises.

[1] Sozomen, viii. 19.   [2] A.D. 172. Eusebius, v. 16.

But though it took its name from Montanus, and he was believed to be the inspired director of its course, yet the real secret of its existence was, that its members claimed to be men who acted truly upon those rules which all Christians professed to reverence; that, in proof of it, they exercised extraordinary self-denial; and that no gross sin had stained their baptismal purity. A single gross sin was enough to exclude men from this select body. Many practices, which other Christians thought allowable, were by them renounced. They enjoined greater reserve in dress and in manners; and no one who was engaged in second marriage could be admitted to their ranks.

If this exclusive spirit had not been grounded in some deep principle, it would soon have passed away, when it was found, contrary to the expectations of Montanus, that no manifestations of that especial power to which he pretended could be proved to continue with his sect.[1] Yet it maintained its ground, and shewed the real cause of its vitality by its union with another body of malcontents, who discovered themselves eighty years later in Christ's kingdom. After the time of Antoninus, the Christians had enjoyed a long period of comparative tranquillity, during which there was little to put the reality of their principles to the test. At length, when their numbers had mightily increased, while ancient discipline and the strictness of early faith had suffered melancholy decay, the persecution of Decius burst upon them like a thunder-storm.[2] The Church contained many who, living in the midst of a heathen population, had in heart participated in heathen crimes. Could it be expected that those who would not live for Christ, should be ready on a sudden to die for His name? Nothing but the strictness of a self-denying life could prepare men for the crown of martyrdom. Many doubtless were found watching, and gave proofs of a faith

---

[1] The argument of Asterius Urbanus against the Montanists. Eus. v. 16. p. 231.   [2] A.D. 250.

of which, in these days of rest and ease, we have no example. But the martyr Cyprian gives this picture of the Church at large: "Men's study has been to increase their property; they have been swallowed up by covetousness, forgetting the duty of believers, and the example of the apostolic age. Bishops have been without devotion, and priests without sincerity; their works without mercy, their manners without discipline. Marriages with the heathen have corrupted the members of Christ. Not only have oaths been frequent, but even perjuries. Men in office have been proud, evil-speaking, and contentious. Many bishops, whose voice and example ought to have been a warning, despising their divine office, leaving their posts and deserting their people, have wandered forth in search of worldly gain."[1] When the time of trial came upon such men, how immediate must be their downfall! And so it proved. "They did not wait," says the same holy man, "till they might be summoned to deny, or brought by force before the altars of incense. Many were vanquished before the conflict, and fell before the fight. They did not even leave themselves the opportunity of appearing reluctant. They ran willingly to the Forum, they hastened spontaneously to destruction, as though it had long been their desire, as though they were embracing an opportunity which they had always coveted. What shall I say of those whom the magistrates had to defer, because evening prevented their sacrifice—who even entreated that their ruin might not be delayed? How can such men pretend that they were compelled to sin, when they rather put compulsion on their seducers?"[2]

Such was the general picture. But there were some whose spirits were stirred within them at the common degeneracy. Among these was Novatian, a distinguished presbyter of the Roman Church. His course had been one well fitted for the development of an extraordinary spirit. Brought up a

[1] De Lapsis. [2] Cyprian de Lapsis, p. 171.

gentile, he had sought among the schools of philosophy [1] for the resolution of those doubts which exercised the minds of reflecting heathens. But he had sought in vain from philosophy what philosophy could not supply. Thus circumstanced, he had been afflicted by a mental disease, either common insanity or the influence of an evil spirit, from which he was relieved through the Church's office by exorcism.[2] His superior promise is afterwards attested by his ordination—a privilege not allowed in common to those who, like him, had been baptised in sickness, and who were therefore presumed to have delayed their conversion. After his ordination, he declined the common duties of the ministry, and betook himself to "another pursuit,"—holy thought, namely, and ascetic mortification.

From this state he was called by those who, feeling or professing similar views, formed themselves into that exclusive party to which the evils of the time gave occasion. Could they unite again with men whose ready renunciation of Christ proved the insincerity of their allegiance? Was this the Lord's kingdom, so magnificently portrayed in ancient prophecy? Was this the host, "terrible as an army with banners,"—this body of weak friends and concealed enemies? It was impossible,[3] they maintained, for those who had fallen so readily to be again received among the soldiers of Christ. God might, indeed, pardon, and Christ might hereafter accept them, because washed by His blood: but to receive them into the Church would be to forfeit its claim to be Christ's kingdom, the city of God here below.

Thus was a division again made in the body of the Church. The Novatians formed a distinct communion, a Church within the Church, adhering to the same faith and order, and considering the same sacraments to be the appointed means of grace, but confining Christ's kingdom to

---

[1] Cyprian, Ep. 52.   [2] Euseb. vi. 43.
[3] Socrates, i. 10. Pacian, iii. § 1.

those who, since their baptism, had never been guilty of any open sin. They too had their stricter[1] life to oppose to the less precise enactments of the Church Catholic; and the attractive appearance of a communion of consistent Christians, and the name of Puritans, gained them many adherents. Why did they forget that the Gospel net had included bad as well as good within its folds, and that it must leaven the whole lump of this wide-spread world? Did the fifth empire lose its title to a kingdom, any more than the four preceding, because traitors were at times found among its subjects? Did they not know that human motives are known to the Searcher of hearts alone, and that here, therefore, no care will secure the Church's purity? This exclusive spirit had a necessary tendency to produce pride and self-sufficiency in themselves, while their refusal to extend the ordinances of the Church to so many, whom they still encouraged to hope for salvation, was not unlikely to lead men to look for other grounds of confidence than the Spirit's help and the blood of the Redeemer.

Recommended, however, by its appearance of sanctity, this sect extended itself widely; and it took especial root in Phrygia,[2] where it united with the remnant of the Montanists.[3] It gained great head likewise in the luxurious city of Constantinople, where, after a time, it put on a more court-like garb, and its bishops became favourites with senators[4] and emperors. But the especial ground of its increase was that the Church was suffering at this season under the distractions of heresy. This was just the period when it was rent by those divisions respecting our Lord's nature which were introduced by the Arians. Had it been possible to point to a united communion, existing without difference or division throughout the world, the petty pretensions of the scattered Novatians would have lost that hold on men's imaginations, from which they derived all

---

[1] Sozomen, vii. 18.   [2] Socrates, v. 21, 22.
[3] Pacian, ii. § 3.   [4] Socrates, vi. 22.

Early Schismatics—Montanus and Novatian. 181

their strength. When the Arian heresy, therefore, had in a measure passed away, or at all events had been driven without the Church's gates, the Novatians rapidly declined. Small as were their comparative numbers, they could not escape inward divisions.[1] They fell before those arguments, drawn from the unity of Christ's kingdom, which are so forcibly directed against them by Pacian, bishop of Barcelona. They had attempted to shew, by an appeal to reasoning, that the characteristics of the Church were found only with themselves; the body of Christ,[2] they argued, could consist of none save the pure. He met them by an appeal to history and to facts. He shewed them, that a system which was historically false could not be logically true. "My name," he said, "is Christian; my surname is Catholic." "Did no one till the time of Decius understand the meaning of our Lord?"[3] "The Church of Christ,"[4] you tell me, "is a people born of water and of the Holy Ghost. Well then, who has closed from me the divine fountain? Who has deprived me of the gift of the Holy Ghost? Have not we the living water which springs from Christ, and is it not *you* who have withdrawn yourselves from the perpetual fountain of your spiritual life? The Spirit does not leave the Church, the great mother of mankind. From whence did *you* gain it? Whence had your own people the gift of the Holy Ghost, save through the medium of her appointed ministers?"

He then points to the fulfilment of ancient prophecy, as illustrated in the wide dominion of the Church. "Number, if you can, the hosts of Catholics,[5] and tell the swarms

---

[1] Socrates, v. 22.
[2] Ep. iii. § 2.
[3] Ep. i. § 4.
[4] Ep. iii. § 2, 3.
[5] A friend suggests, that since there are some persons who, notwithstanding the example set them in the prayer-book, identify the words *Catholic* and *Romanist*, it is necessary to observe, that in the time of Pacian the errors of popery had not appeared, or at least had not been formed into a system; and that the Reformed Catholics of the Church of England claim to be in communion with those of the primitive

of our people. I appeal not merely to the universal belief of every country, but to that which meets you in the adjoining cities. How many do you meet of ours, yourself solitary? And can the seed of Abraham, more numerous than the stars or than the sand of the shore, be verified in your scanty numbers? 'In thee shall all nations of the earth be blessed.' Is this fulfilled by Novatian? Surely our Lord is not so ill supplied with followers, nor was it for so small a body that He shed His blood. Come, then, my brethren, behold the Church of God enlarging her tents, stretching right and left her stakes and cords; and understand that God's name must be glorified from the rising to the setting of the sun."[1]

These reasonings for a time prevailed. The separating parties, after existing till the end of the fourth century, gradually melted again into the unity of the Church, and renewed their allegiance to the spiritual kingdom. Thus was division checked, to reappear after the corruption and tyranny of Rome had so completely broken up the Church's concord, that such arguments could no longer be adduced with equal truth, or accepted with equal confidence.

Church, from whose doctrines and order they consider the Catholics to have departed. Surely it is deeply to be regretted that any members of the Church Catholic in this country should be so ignorant, or so inconsistent, as virtually to declare that they are not Christians, by sanctioning the Romanists in their usurpation of the name of Catholics.

[1] Ep. iii. 25, 27.

THE CHURCH'S VICTORY. CONSTANTINE. THE FIFTH KINGDOM.

Reign of Diocletian — Marcellus — Persecution — Martyrs in Palestine—Constantine—Vision of the Cross—The Worldly Power Chosen to Behold it—Christ's Kingdom Established.

> "And when she list pour forth her larger spright,
> She would command the hasty sun to stay,
> Or backward turn his course from heaven's height:
> Sometimes great hosts of men she could dismay;
> Dryshod to pass, she parts the floods in tway."—SPENSER.

AND now the time was come for a great change in the system of the world. By sure, though unseen degrees, the grain of mustard-seed had arisen, till its size promised to overshadow the earth. In the long interval of rest which followed the Decian persecution,[1] the Church of Christ had so increased in influence and numbers, that the heathen looked upon it no less with fear than astonishment. By the end of the third century, it was manifest that nothing but some mighty effort could prevent the cross from triumphing over the altars of paganism. If the blood-cemented fabric of heathen worship was to endure, it must be by the destruction of a system too formidable to be any longer slighted.

At this season it pleased God, who makes storms as well as sunshine the ministers of His will, to set a prince over the Roman empire, whose sagacity enabled him to employ all the resources of human policy for the overthrow of the Church. The Emperor Diocletian[2] had given new life to the vast body over which he reigned, and his wise plans of worldly government made him a second Augustus,—a re-founder of the Roman state. One thing only seemed to him to be wanting. What his heart desired, was the restoration of the ancient system[3] of his country; and of this, its original superstitions were an essential part. For they

---

[1] A.D. 250. [2] A.D. 285. Gibbon, cap. 13. [3] Euseb. viii. 17.

were bound up with that which had been one secret of
Rome's ascendency—the unshaken confidence in a fate
which watched over the eternity of the empire. But as their
restoration could not be effected by reason, it must be accomplished by force. Now, then, came the conflict which
was to decide the history of the world. For a little hour
the victory seemed in suspense—while paganism and the
Church were entwined in the death-struggle together. The
eyes of all men were on the event; for the fall of Dagon was
not as of old, in darkness and silence,—it was acted on the
middle stage of earth—its scene-plot was the Roman empire.
The Church of God had emerged from Babylonish bondage,
and flourished under Persian protection; it had spread
through the channels of Grecian civilisation, and now it was
to exact homage from the majesty of Rome; it had
trampled on the pride of the Stoics, and contemned the
alluring arts of Epicurus; and now it defied the swords of
thirty legions, and the arm which swayed from Euphrates to
the ocean.

The Emperor Diocletian was long withheld by feelings of
humanity from commencing that struggle, which was to end
in the establishment of the kingdom of Christ. At length,
his affection to the ancient system was reinforced by the
arguments of his son-in-law Galerius, who was addicted, not
only by policy, but by hereditary[1] affection, to the old
superstition. Galerius found the old man the more ready
to admit his sanguinary councils, because he had lately felt
himself rebuked by the presence of some Christian officers
of his army or household. While he sacrificed, some
attendant Christians signed themselves with the cross, in
token that they bore no part in the impiety; and the im-
pure spirits, whose aid the heathen sought, and often really
obtained, were chased away by the holy token.[2] Inflamed
with anger, Diocletian had required all who bore offices in
the court or army to take part in heathen sacrifices;—an

[1] Lact. de M. P. xi.   [2] *Ibid.*

order which induced many Christians to abandon their hopes of preferment, and retire to private stations; while some, not allowed this escape, died as martyrs to the faith.[1] The connexion of heathen superstition with the public events of life, often made a banquet or a festival the decisive moment when such self-sacrifice was suddenly required. Thus, Marcellus, who had risen to the office of centurion, was celebrating the emperor's birthday, when he was called upon to take part in an idolatrous service, from which the soldiery had hitherto been exempt.[2] But this brave man, though knowing that the result must be the loss of his office, and probably of his life, hesitated not between God and mammon. "Taking off his military belt, 'I am the soldier,' he said, 'of Christ, the eternal King.' Then throwing down his arms, and the vine-bough, his emblem of office, 'From this time,' he exclaimed, 'I am no soldier of your emperors: your gods of wood and stone I refuse to adore, for they are deaf and dumb idols. *If such is the condition of soldiers*,[3] that they are compelled to offer sacrifice to the heathen gods and to their emperors, I lay down my vine and belt, I renounce my standard, I refuse to serve."

The execution of this undaunted soldier of Christ (at Tangier in Africa) was but a prelude to similar scenes, in which women, aged men, and striplings were shortly to bear part. After his victory over the Persians, Galerius spent a winter with Diocletian in the palace at Nicomedia; and the result of their secret consultations[4] was, that the aged prince at length abandoned his irresolution, and agreed to quench the flame of Christianity by the blood of its professors. In the very same year,[5] therefore, which witnessed the last Roman triumph—that insulting sign of contempt for the

---

[1] Euseb. viii. 4.   [2] Ruinart's "Act. Mart." A.D. 298.

[3] These words evidently imply the new condition at this time exacted from soldiers, and probably first exacted on the feast of the emperor's birthday, just as the decree against Christianity was afterwards published at Easter.

[4] A.D. 303.   [5] Lact. de. M. P. xvii.

miseries of mankind—began the last and greatest persecution against the Christians.

The feast of the Roman god Terminus,[1] who presided over boundaries, had been selected to be the day beyond which Christianity should be unknown. With its earliest dawn, the splendid church which was built in so conspicuous a part of Nicomedia as even to overhang the palace, was unexpectedly surrounded by the soldiery, who burst into it —curious to witness under what shape was worshipped the Christian God—seized the copies of the Scriptures, and whatever else was to be found, and demolished the building. The Christians, just preparing to celebrate the holy season of Easter,[2] were overwhelmed by the sudden appearance of decrees, which required the destruction of their churches, the surrender of all copies of the Scriptures, and deprived themselves of all the rights of citizens, and of the protection of the law. Other enactments immediately followed, by which, first the bishops and clergy, and then all private Christians, were enjoined to sacrifice to idols, on pain of confiscation, imprisonment, torture, and death.

And now began a scene such as the world has never since witnessed, even in those days when popish tyranny dyed itself red in the blood of martyrs. The horrors of that season are not to be estimated so much by the numbers who perished, though the lowest computation would make them exceed fifteen thousand persons,[3] as by the attendant circumstances of barbarity and outrage. At various times

---

[1] Lact. de M. P. xii.   [2] Eus. viii. 17, p. 406.

[3] Palestine is 156 miles long, and 46 broad. (Reland's "Palestine.") This would give 7176 square miles, or less than $\frac{1}{12}$ part of the Roman empire, which contained 1,600,000 square miles. (Gibbon, i. p. 46.) In Palestine, Eusebius numbers up ninety-two persons put to death. He does not say, though probably he may have meant, that no persons perished except those with whose names he was acquainted. He expressly mentions other places [the Thebaid] where the persecution was far more bloody than in Palestine. Taking Palestine, however, as our standard, and excluding one quarter of the empire as having been

in the history of the Reformation, the persecuted party repelled force by force; and when they were defeated, much blood was shed without mercy. But these massacres, where the conquerors destroyed those whom they feared, or took revenge on those whom they hated, were but the ordinary display of men's violent passions. The deliberate selection of one after another out of an unresisting population; their public exposure, in cold blood, to every kind of ignominy and torture, till human nature sunk under the struggle—this resembles rather the ferocity of those savage beasts whom the persecutors employed as their ministers. Eusebius, who has related in detail the sufferings of ninety-two martyrs within the narrow limits of Palestine, where he was living at the time, speaks of two hundred and twenty-seven men, who were sentenced to its mines after some bodily mutilation.[1] Many had lost an eye, many a foot, or other parts of their body; and for years did men survive in the Church with these tokens of their sincerity. Neither rank nor sex was an exemption. Christian women[2] were subjected but to more intolerable insult; and persons of wealth and of the highest birth perished in the midst of tortures. Eusebius, professing to speak only of the clergy of the principal cities,[3] mentions eleven[4] bishops in his own pro-

comparatively free from persecution, the number of martyrs would come to nearly fifteen thousand four hundred. It is true that the persecution lasted longer in Palestine than elsewhere, but we are nowhere told it was more bloody; and nearly half the martyrs who perished there were put to death in one year, as though to try the effect of such severity in striking terror into the rest. The same experiment was probably made in other places, and equally without effect.

[1] De Mar. Pal. viii. [2] Eus. de Mar. Pal. v. [3] Eus. viii. 13.

[4] If Mr Gibbon's usual sagacity had not been extinguished by his hatred to Christianity, he could not have been guilty of so gross an error as to say, that "from the pen of Eusebius it may be collected, that only nine bishops were punished with death;" cap. xvi. ii. 493. For, first, Eusebius does not profess to mention all the bishops martyred, but only such as presided over chief cities; viii. 13. Secondly, Eusebius expressly mentions twelve, and not nine, cases of this kind.

vinces and the nearer part of Egypt, besides the Bishop of Nicomedia, who perished in the persecution ; and those who, after suffering tortures, were allowed to live, were degraded to the most menial offices.[1]

Meantime all the churches were destroyed throughout the wide limits of the Roman empire; and to a superficial observer it might have appeared that the religion of half mankind had been suppressed in a moment. So thought the emperor, and in his pride recorded his victory in monumental inscriptions, which have survived as witnesses of his defeat. His haughty boast was, that "the name of Christians, the destroyers of the republic, is abolished, and their superstition everywhere destroyed." [2]

Even Constantius, who, with the title of Cæsar, ruled under the emperor in Gaul and Britain, joined in the de-

---

Thirdly, it is obvious that Eusebius, who does not profess to give a complete list even of the bishops martyred in chief cities, was confining himself to the neighbourhood which he himself inhabited ; for except Nicomedia, the capital, every bishop of whom he speaks belonged to Syria or Egypt.

Equally unfounded is the assertion, that Adauctus was "the only person of rank or distinction who appears to have suffered death during this persecution ;" Gib. § xvi. vol. ii. 480. It is sufficient to mention Philomorus and Phileas, Eus. viii. 9 ; the governor of the town in Phrygia, *id.* viii. 11 ; five women of noble birth, *id.* viii. 12 ; Appianus, Eus. de Mar. Pal. iv. And the enumeration of Eusebius does not profess to go beyond Palestine.

[1] Eus. de Mar. Pal. xii.

[2] "This inscription may be read," says Baronius, "on a magnificent column at Clunia, in Spain." [Near Aranda, on the Douro.]

"'Diocletian surnamed Jupiter, Maximian surnamed Hercules, Cæsar's Augustus's—in memory of the augmentation of the Roman empire, both in the East and West, and of the utter extinction of the name of Christians, who were overthrowing the Republic.'

"Again : another inscription in the same place has this meaning :

"'Diocletian Cæsar Augustus — in memory of the adoption of Galerius in the East, of the universal extinction of the superstition of Christ, and of the extension of the worship of the gods.'

"The same thing may be read at Arevacum in Spain, in various columns."—BARONIUS, iii. ann. 304, § ix.

struction of the Christian temples; though that more precious temple of the Holy Ghost, the bodies of Christians, his humanity forbade him to violate.[1] Even in Britain, however, we read of the martyrdom of St. Alban; while in other parts of the world, the achievements of many distinguished martyrs are recorded,—as of St. Agnes, of Adauctus, Philomorus, and Phileas, who were celebrated for their rank; and of Lucian of Antioch, and Pamphilus of Tyre, who were known for their abilities and learning.

In the East the persecution continued, with slight intermission, during a space of ten years. Towards the end of that period a famine and pestilence was added to the other evils which afflicted Palestine; and the kindness of the Christians towards the sick and destitute[2] induced the heathen to respect a faith which could render men as charitable and indulgent towards their brethren, as they had shewn themselves patient and unbending in their Master's service.

But the time was come when God would avenge His own elect,[3] though He had borne long. Diocletian and Galerius were now removed from the stage; the first had for some time resigned the sovereignty, the second was dead. Diocletian had divided the empire into four parts, each entrusted to a separate ruler, the elder having the chief place; and at this time the East was governed by Maximin and Licinius, Italy and Africa by Maxentius, while Constantine had succeeded his father Constantius in Gaul and Britain. But these several chiefs were not on friendly terms with one another, and were secretly looking round for means by which they might secure themselves or destroy their rivals. Meanwhile the persecution had in great measure ceased, except in the dominions of Maximin, who ruled over the south-eastern parts of the empire. But the discerning mind of Constantine, when considering from what quarter he should derive support, perceived something in the Christian

[1] Lactant. de M. P.   [2] Eus. ix. 8.   [3] A.D. 311.

system which might not only be harmless to those who tolerated, but beneficial to those who protected it. The words of his friendly biographer, Eusebius, as well as his own subsequent conduct, would lead us to suppose him actuated rather by an immediate sense of worldly advantage than by the expectation of spiritual good.[1] It was avowedly when considering how he might gain support for his military designs, that he "began to consider what god he could enrol as a champion on his side. In his inquiries, the thought arose, how many, who had before grasped the sovereign power, and had given their affiance and offered sacrifices to the gods of the heathen, had failed, after being flattered with delusive hopes."

Constantine may afterwards have attained to deeper and better thoughts, but in this manner was he first determined to implore succour from the Christian's God. And thus was the spectacle again brought round, of which in the days of Nebuchadnezzar there had been a short-lived example. There had then been the promise of an union between the majesty of human rule and the supremacy of God's dominion,—the chief of human beings calling on his subjects to join with him in honouring that God whose prophet he had learnt to reverence. In the hour of that first monarchy's highest ascendency, it had touched upon the Church of God, and such sense of inferiority had been the consequence. It had seemed as though the two might ally; as though that human system, which had so long dissevered itself from the religious principle, had met it again and recognised its master; as though Noah's prediction, which spoke of the wide-spreading power of man as taking up its abode in God's Church, was at once to be consummated. But such meeting was but for a season. It was not given to that empire, which had been originally reared by the children of Ham, to be the immediate prototype of Messiah's kingdom. The prophecies had gathered them-

[1] Vita Constan. i. 27.

selves into shape and order, but they passed away for one of the days of heaven. And now, when a thousand years had elasped, and when those empires had run their course, which were announced at the previous era, the same combination of circumstances reappears. But now the world's dominion has centred in the race of Japheth, ere it comes in contact with that spiritual principle which had been enshrined in the family of Shem. And, as at the former epoch, it is the earthly power which requires the Church's aid. Nebuchadnezzar found contentment from the Jewish prophet; and so the world-pervading might of Christianity is invoked by an emperor who feels how hollow and unreal a security is the purple of Rome. The Babylonish monarch, the foremost man of that era at which the first empire came to its height, and from which the course of the three following was distinctly viewed, is himself chosen to behold the vision which foreshadows the course of God's coming providence. And this analogy gives great confirmation to a circumstance which historical evidence distinctly testifies, that when God's dealings had an end, and the destined career of the four empires was completed, it was, in like manner, to the possessor of the sovereign state that the vision was revealed, which indicated the nature of their consummation. For this was the declaration of the first Christian emperor of Rome, just as, a thousand years before, the vision of its greatness had mixed with the dreams of Nebuchadnezzar. "As I was meditating," says Constantine,[1] "on my situation, and imploring God's help, this wonderful vision was presented to me. Mid-day being a little past, I saw with these eyes, in that part of the heaven just above the sun, the figure of a cross of light, and with it these words, *By this prevail*. And when I much doubted, Christ appeared to me the selfsame night in a dream, and ordered me to form a standard like that

---

[1] A.D. 312. Vita Cons. i. 28.

which I had seen, and to employ it as my defence against my enemies."[1]

By whatever means this intimation was conveyed, Constantine yielded it prompt obedience. He took the cross as his standard in his wars against his various opponents. One by one they fell before him. After conquering Maxentius,[2] and thus becoming master of Italy and all the west, he was opposed to Licinius, who in like manner had united all the east under his power. As Constantine appealed to the God of Christians, so did Licinius to the heathen powers. After conquering Maximin, Licinius had in some degree renewed the persecution of the Christians.[3] And now he was about to measure himself against the champion whom the God of battles had raised up for their support. "This hour, he exclaimed, "shall decide which of us has been in error.[4] It shall be umpire between our gods, and Him whom our adversary honours."[5] So, too, felt Constantine. The standard of the Christian faith was guarded by an especial band of soldiers, and committed to the care of a chosen warrior.[6] Wherever it appeared, the enemy were scattered in flight. But the emperor's attention was especially drawn to the circumstance, that the chosen standard-bearer had no sooner, from cowardice, resigned his trust than he fell a victim to the fate he sought to avoid.[7] Constantine's victory was complete: and while it made him the sole head of the Roman world, it determined the still more important point, that Christianity was to be the established belief of the empire.

Henceforth, then, with one short exception, we see its princes bringing their power and honour into the Church of Christ. Constantine declared, that while he recognised those bishops who had authority from God for the Church's inward conduct, he felt that, for its outward protection, he

---

[1] Vita Cons. i. 29.   [2] A.D. 313.   [3] Vita Cons. ii. 2.
[4] A.D. 323.   [5] Vita Cons. ii. 5.
[6] Ibid. ii. 7, 8.   [7] Ibid. ii. 9.

also had a like episcopal or superintending power.[1] Some time, however, expired before the might of human society could do its work in rendering full homage to the institution of God. Not till towards the end of this century were the forms of paganism finally superseded by the Church of Christ. Meanwhile the fourth empire had not done all its work. The Church had grown up within it till her lordly boughs had overtopped the decaying bulwarks of the dungeon which threatened her destruction. But still the mouldering fabric had some service to render towards the immortal plant which had overpowered it, and then its relics must be scattered towards the winds of heaven.

―――o―――

THE CHURCH SYSTEM CEMENTED. THE CREEDS.

Interval of Tranquillity—Arian Controversy—Constantine—Vain Effort to Obviate Discussion—Council Summoned at Nice—Arians Silenced—Their Political Intrigues—Theodosius—Council of Constantinople—Approach of Barbarians—Impending Destruction of the Roman Empire—Its Final Homage to the Fifth Empire—Close of Ancient History.

> "Still glides the stream, and shall not cease to glide.
>   The form remains, the function never dies;
>   While we the brave, the mighty, and the wise,
> We men, who in our morn of youth defied
>   The elements, must vanish; be it so,—
> Enough if something from our hands have power
> To live, and act, and serve the future hour;
>   And if, as toward the silent tomb we go,
> Through love, through hope, and faith's transcendent dower,
>   We feel that we are greater than we know."—WORDSWORTH.

CONSTANTINE'S greatest service to the Church has been said to be that, by assembling the first general council at Nice, he afforded it an opportunity for laying

[1] Vita Cons. iv. 24.

down fixed rules of doctrine and discipline. If this was the judgment of Epiphanius[1] but a few years after the death of Constantine, how much more strongly would the same truth have been impressed upon him, could he have foreseen the events which were coming on the world,— could he have known that the age of Constantine was to be followed by that mighty overthrow which ended the supremacy of Rome! For then were the sun and moon darkened, the powers which rule this lower world were shaken from their seat, and the whole fabric of human society was changed. Those countries where the faith bore rule were occupied by savage tribes from the ends of the earth, and the very languages in which our Lord had heretofore been worshipped were done away. Henceforth Christendom was divided among so many nations, that never since that time have its bishops assembled with one consent, for the confirmation of truth or the removal of error; nor is it likely that they will again meet, till they are all gathered to render an account of their stewardship before the Son of man.

How important was it that this interval should be duly used, and that a fixed creed, and a concordant practice, should preserve the unity of the faith among the various and unconnected tribes of modern Christendom! The fifth empire was, indeed, to be unlike the other four: it needed no human hands to shape it; its principle was not worldly subjection, but community of faith and worship. But how could it be an empire at all, what principles of truth or agreement could survive, unless, before the opportunity of conference had passed away, its principles had received that public acknowledgment of which our creeds are a lasting declaration? These creeds had existed, indeed, before the time of Constantine; they were built upon a basis as ancient as the first century; but during times of persecution they could not be publicly declared, or receive

[1] Quoted by Lardner, iv. 60.

The Church System Cemented—The Creeds.

the public sanction of the collected Church. This, therefore, was the great step which it was enabled to take by the protection of Constantine; and this was the crowning blessing which it derived from the preparation made for it by the fourth empire.

Constantine, however, as little contemplated this great object, as Nebuchadnezzar did the declaration of those mighty plans, which his connection with the Church of old unfolded. When he conquered Maxentius,[1] and published the edict of Milan, by which the Christians were relieved from persecution, he thought apparently that he was joining a body which was perfectly at unity in itself. But when by the conquest of Licinius, ten years later,[2] he added the East also to his empire, he found that the Christian world was not absolutely free from that division by which the heathen were so much afflicted. His attention was called particularly to a dispute which distracted the Church of Alexandria; and he sent Hosius, a distinguished Spanish bishop, who had been a confessor (*i.e.*, had suffered torture) during the late persecutions, to allay it. He bade the disputants remember that the questions which divided them might as well be left undecided; or, if they were entertained in secret as injurious speculations, ought at all events not to be brought forward to the annoyance of others.[3] "Agree, both of you, to admit a supreme Providence, to cultivate love and kindness, and to free me from anxiety and doubt."[4]

Happy was it for the whole Church, and for all future generations, that the bishop of Alexandria at that eventful era was a man who judged things by a scriptural standard, and knew that tranquillity cannot permanently prevail, unless it is founded in truth. Of the temper of Arius, by whom the offensive novelties were introduced, Alexander the bishop had enjoyed previous experience. Arius had

---

[1] A.D. 313.
[2] A.D. 323.
[3] Euseb. Vita Cons. xi. 69.
[4] Ib. 71, 72.

been brought up in the school of Lucian at Antioch, out of which issued most of the chief supporters of his errors. Their master Lucian seems not to have shared the opinions of his disciples;[1] but either an irreverent spirit had directed their enquiries, or they had been infected by the external influences of their place of education; for Antioch was the most luxurious city of the empire. And now the restored peace of the Church gave these Collucianists, as they called themselves, an opportunity of questioning those truths which had been most uniformly believed among Christians. The attack was commenced by Arius, who, after having previously given proofs of insubordination, had been received on repentance as a presbyter of the Church of Alexandria; but he was supported by abler partisans, especially by his old companion Eusebius, bishop of Nicomedia. Eusebius the historian, intimately connected with the Church at Antioch, was to a certain extent also infected by his sentiments.

Had Alexander yielded when Arius began to blaspheme the Divine Word,—had he allowed that the deity of the Son of God was an uncertain matter, on which every one might safely have his own opinion,—how would he have been fulfilling his office as a witness to that "form of sound words," which had been handed down to him from the apostles? The principles of Arius, as was afterwards more fully explained, implied that our Lord's supremacy meant nothing but that in Him was manifested a more especial measure of that divine power which might in various ways be communicated to any creature. Thus the reverence for Him, as having of right that place which He claimed, would have been lost,—a mere arbitrary sentence would have been supposed to have conferred upon Him what was not naturally His due. This was not the system which Alexander had received from his predecessors; and therefore whatever offence he might give to politicians or worldly rulers, who

[1] Bull, Diss. Fid. Nic. ii. 13, § 7.

The Church System Cemented—The Creeds. 197

thought that to minister to the civil tranquillity was the highest office of the Church, he would not allow them to be propagated in her fold. At first he attempted to argue with the innovator. But Arius was well stored with logical subtleties, which he opposed to the established doctrine of the Christian community.[1] The bishop, perceiving, as he declares,[2] that "the Church's body was but one, and that it was necessary to hand on the bond of unity," excluded the offending member from his communion, and esteemed even the emperor's wishes of less moment than the truth.

If Constantine, therefore, would preserve that harmony, which he especially desired to cultivate among his Christian subjects, it could only be by invoking some authority to which the Church deferred. The only such authority was in the bishops, to whom, as the successors of the apostles, our Lord had given in common the government of His people. Their office constituted them the natural witnesses of what truths had been received from the beginning. But as no one had as yet risen up in the Church who had even laid claim to that authority over his brother bishops which was afterwards usurped by the pope, there was none but Constantine himself who could call them together.[3] This he did, not as an ecclesiastical functionary, but by means of his civil power. Thus did the might of human society lend its aid to the Church of God, and the prince called together his subjects to agree on those decisions to which he should himself submit. The object was not merely to determine the question of Arianism, but also to adjust any other differences which might exist in the Church, that "those who differed in any point from the great body of Christians might be brought into unity with their brethren."[4] Nice in Bithynia was fixed for the place of meeting; and to it came bishops not only from the adjoining district, but from every part of the Christian world. "From all the Churches

[1] Soc. i. 5.   [2] Socrates, i. 6.   [3] Euseb. Vita Constan. iii. 5.
[4] Soc. v. 22. p. 298.

of Europe, Africa, and Asia, the most distinguished servants of God assembled. Within the precincts of one house of prayer were seen Syrians and Cilicians, men of Phenicia and Palestine, of Egypt and Libya. With these came a Persian bishop, and another from Scythia. Pontus and Asia, Phrygia and Pamphylia, sent their best. Others came from Thrace and Macedonia, from Achaia and Epirus, and the regions beyond."[1] The decrees of the council were attested likewise by bishops from Gaul. "From Spain came that distinguished man (the confessor Hosius) to take his place among the rest. The bishop of Rome was absent on account of his great age, but he sent presbyters to represent him."[2]

The 318 bishops who assembled on this occasion were felt to represent so completely the judgment of the whole Church, that the resolutions which they passed were dispersed and accepted even beyond the limits of the Roman empire. Their representation of the ancient tenets of the Church was further strengthened by Acesius,[3] a Novatian bishop, who, by Constantine's favour, was introduced to their deliberations. He bore witness to the fact, that what they had agreed upon was the immemorial principle of the Church, from which his party had for more than half a century been divided. The emperor asked him why he dissented from the Church, if he admitted its doctrine. He explained his system, that those who had once fallen, could not be received again to the full participation of Christian privileges, and that he could not communicate with a body, which admitted members whose piety there had been reason to question. "Take a ladder, Acesius," said the emperor, "and mount up into heaven by yourself."[4]

But what gave the greatest authority to this council, was the number of bishops who had proved their sincerity by their sufferings in the late persecutions, and who still bore

[1] Soc. i. 8.
[2] Ib. i. 8.
[3] Athen. ad. Apos. § 2, p. 892.
[4] Soc. i. 10.

about them "the marks of the Lord Jesus." "A whole throng of martyrs might be seen gathered together. There was Paulus, bishop of Neocæsarea, who had suffered from the cruelty of Licinius, and was maimed both in his hands and feet by burning irons. Others had lost their right eyes, or their right feet; of these was Paphnutius, an Egyptian bishop;"[1] the same whose opposition defeated the design of imposing celibacy on the priesthood.[2] Many distinguished laymen, too, were present, who, though they took no part in the proceedings, yet were attracted by the importance of the occasion. One of them, himself a confessor, was listening to some preparatory discussions, before the general meeting of the council, in which an attempt was made to decide the great questions before them by logical acuteness; as though the object of the council was to deduce new opinions, instead of giving testimony to the fact of what had always been believed. Unable to bear such perversion of the truth, he broke in upon the disputants with an earnestness which effectually silenced them, exclaiming: "It was not an array of syllogisms, nor a vain subtlety, which was delivered to us by our Lord and His apostles, but a bare doctrine, of which faith and a holy conversation must be the guard."[3]

The same view of the Christian doctrine, as a transmitted depository of revealed truths, was still more manifest in the answer of a confessor—an old man of simple character, and altogether unpractised in the arts of disputation—to a heathen philosopher, who was employing his powers of raillery to embarrass some of the assembled bishops by questions to which it was impossible to reply. "When the old man seemed about to answer, some thoughtless persons who knew him were ready to mock, while the better part were fearful lest he should expose himself to ridicule in the unequal contest. Yet they felt that a man of such a reverent character must not be opposed, if he chose to speak. 'In

[1] Theod. i. 7. [2] Soc. i. 11. [3] Soc. i. 8.

the name of Jesus Christ,' he said, 'philosopher, attend! There is one God, Maker of heaven and earth, and of all things visible and invisible, who hath created all things by the power of His Word, and hath upheld them by the sanctification of His Spirit. This Word, which we call the Son, in pity to man's errors and degradation, chose to be born of a woman, to converse among men, and to die for them. And He shall come again, as the Judge of each man's actions. Such, without admitting of controversy, is our creed. Trifle not, therefore, by asking for arguments of that which faith establishes, or by searching into the manner in which this can or cannot be effected. But if you believe, answer me, and allow it.' The philosopher, confounded, replied, 'I believe.' And, feeling thankful for his defeat, he became a convert to the aged confessor, and counselled the like to those who had formerly argued with him; declaring solemnly that his mind had been changed by no human power, but that some inexplicable influence had compelled him to become a Christian."[1]

This reverent attachment to their ancient system pervaded the whole council. When the Arians attempted to argue against that "form of sound words" which had been handed down among them, they "would not even hear their propositions,"[2] but rejected all reasonings against the faith as blasphemous. A confession, which the Arians offered in opposition to the ancient creeds, had no sooner been read than it was, with one consent, torn to pieces and rejected.[3] But although the fathers knew well what doctrine they were resolved to maintain, and although they wished for nothing but the perpetuation of the ancient profession of faith, yet to accomplish their purpose required no little sagacity. For they had to do with men, who, professing to agree with them in reverencing the ancient creeds, had invented such interpretations as left the very points ambiguous which they were intended to determine. Some criterion was wanted, to shew

---

[1] Sozomen, i. 18.   [2] Socrates, i. 9.   [3] Theodosius, i. 7.

whether men received not merely the words of the old forms, but their meaning. For this purpose, all scriptural terms were clearly unavailing. For the terms of Scripture each party professed to respect, while they were totally at variance about their meaning. Yet the fathers knew that holy Scripture had one meaning alone; and that its real meaning, the very mind of the Spirit, was that interpretation which from the apostles' days had been received in the Church. The Arians wished for a less positive and fixed belief—for such loose opinions as might harmonise better with any popular system; and the tendency of that age, which had lately escaped from the superstitions of polytheism, was to recognise nothing but the single principle of the Divine unity. They entreated, therefore, that the council would content itself with the use of scriptural expressions, that is, that it would adopt a test, which should leave the very point unsettled which it professed to resolve. Eusebius the historian, whose leaning was rather to the new opinions, produced the ancient creed of his Church of Cæsarea, and asked why they could not be satisfied with its time-honoured expressions.[1] He was answered, that this creed was true, but not sufficient; since it now appeared, that its words could be admitted by those who rejected its acknowledged meaning.

Something, therefore, was wanted, which might be decisive. But when our Lord's character was unfolded, that He was the very Son of the Father; that Deity truly belonged to Him; that He was really the Son of God; and when His attributes were set forth; it might obviously be discerned, by the gestures and looks which were mutually exchanged among the Arian leaders, that they were prepared to assent to any such expressions, but without acknowledging the truth which the orthodox party designed them to convey.[2] And they soon admitted that these expressions

[1] Socrates, i. 8.
[2] Athanasius ad Apos. § i. p. 895. Theod. i. 8.

"gave them no concern," for that men too were in Scripture "said to be gods," were called the sons of God; and that any creature might possess divine power and attributes, in such measure and for such time as they were bestowed upon him. It was then that a new form of words was introduced, by whom suggested we are not informed, though their defence fell doubtless principally upon Athanasius, who, as deacon of the Church of Alexandria, in attendance on his bishop, was in truth the leading spirit of the assembly.[1] The place, honour, and dignity of our Lord were not called in question by the Arians, but these were declared not to have been His natural right, but to have been arbitrarily bestowed upon a creature like ourselves. Now, among the words of the ancients [2] were found some which expressly discriminated our Lord's origin from that of any created being, and declared that He was of *one substance* with the Father. These words, therefore, the fathers took, and associated them to the creed. And their declaration, that our Lord was "very God, *of* very God, of *one substance* with the Father," has ever since continued to be the peculiar guardian of this main article of the faith.

The discussion and acceptance of the Nicene Creed took place in Constantine's own presence, and under his direction, in a hall of his palace. And during the two months that the sittings of the council continued, he provided support for its members, as he also discharged the cost of their journeyings to and from the place of meeting. Through his influence the creed of the council was accepted, not only by the great majority, who heartily received, but even by the small body of Arianising bishops, who at first refused it.[3] And thus did the true faith appear to be established. But political circumstances soon afterwards arose, which, by subjecting the Church to trials, served to test the

---

[1] Socrates, i. 8.
[2] This is admitted by Eusebius. Socrates, i. 8, p. 25.
[3] Ib. i. 8, p. 22.

The Church System Cemented—The Creeds. 203

truth of its principles. Such were the persecutions exercised by Constantine and his sons against those who adhered to the faith of the Nicene Council, when, through the influence of Eusebius of Nicomedia, and other Arian prelates, they determined to undo the work which they had effected. For a time they seemed almost to succeed, and either deceived or overbore the leaders of the Church. Athanasius alone stood firm, when all the world seemed against him. Though five times banished, and often in danger of his life, yet his firmness was in the end the main instrument of Providence for the victory of that faith which God had originally given him wisdom to unfold. At length, when the family of Constantine had passed away, and Theodosius had succeeded to the government of the empire,[1] the principles of the Nicene Council were again permitted to be publicly professed, and soon gained universal concurrence. They needed no ratification, because as the whole Church had already borne its testimony to what it had received from the first, it was impossible that they could have any more complete sanction. It remained only to complete the creed, by determining those questions respecting the Third Person in the blessed Trinity which the Council of Nice had found it unnecessary to consider. The same objections were now urged against this portion of the established doctrine, which had formerly been advanced respecting the Divinity of our blessed Lord. On this account, the second general council met at Constantinople.[2] The ancient creeds[3] had spoken

---

[1] A.D. 379.   [2] A.D. 381.

[3] It has sometimes been inferred, from the silence of the Nicene Council respecting the last clauses in the creed, that the three closing articles, respecting the Catholic Church, forgiveness through the baptismal covenant, and the consequent hope of eternal life, were added at the Council of Constantinople. Bishop Bull, however, has sufficiently proved that these clauses made part of the original creeds of the second century, and were not asserted at Nice, merely because they were not denied. *Vide* Bull *de Necessitate Credendi*, vi. One extract shall be made from this most conclusive work. "I used often to won-

merely in general terms of the Holy Spirit, and had then added those declarations concerning the Catholic Church, the assurance of forgiveness by the baptismal covenant, and the resurrection to another life, which still form the last three clauses in our public belief. The Council of Constantinople inserted those declarations which proclaim the Holy Spirit to be the Lord and Giver of life, and ascribe to Him equal worship and glory with the Father and the Son.

And thus was the great work of building up the Church into one system of doctrine finally effected,[1]—a work for which God's providence seemed to have exactly provided a season, which, if once passed, could never have been recalled. Already was the Roman state tottering to its fall, and with the death of Theodosius it was finally broken up, never to be rejoined.[2] But so completely was the fourth empire destined to be the precursor, which should vanish at the final establishment of Messiah's kingdom, that it was not till the reign of this prince, the last emperor who swayed from east to west, that the Christian was fully substituted for the pagan worship. The altar of victory, which had still

der, that the fathers at Constantinople, after using those terms respecting the Holy Spirit, that He was 'the Lord and Giver of life, which proceedeth from the Father, which, with the Father and the Son, together is worshipped and glorified,' should have added the words, 'who spake by the prophets.' After assigning to the Holy Ghost such magnificent attributes, that He was the Lord, that He bestowed life, that He proceeded from the Father, that He was entitled to the same glory and worship with the Father and the Son, it seemed to me almost a bathos to add that 'He spake by the prophets.' But after I understood that the ancient creed of the Eastern Church had contained the words, 'the Comforter, who spake by the prophets,' I understood that the holy synod had substituted for the word 'Comforter' those magnificent terms, in order that it might more clearly testify the true Deity of the Holy Ghost against Macedonius, and had then added the words, 'who spake by the prophets,' because this was part of the ancient creed."
—§ 12.

[1] The two remaining general councils, at Ephesus and Chalcedon, condemned the Nestorian and Eutychian heresies, but made no alteration in the Creed. [2] A.D. 395.

remained in the Roman senate,[1] was in his days finally condemned; "and the gods of antiquity were dragged in triumph at the chariot-wheels of Theodosius."[2] This work had been begun by Constantine, and he had also been the first to make that formal division of the empire to which the measures of Diocletian tended, by apportioning it among his children. But its separate parts had speedily been reunited under his kinsman, the apostate Julian, who had endeavoured, with the integrity of the empire, to revive its ancient faith. Both the one and the other were finally destroyed by Theodosius, who pronounced the decisive condemnation of paganism; and whose two sons, Arcadius and Honorius, receiving respectively the inheritance of the East and West, consummated the partition of the Roman dominions. This, therefore, is the natural conclusion of ancient history; and thus ended the fourth empire—its task performed.

And now nothing remains but to unfold the fortunes of that fifth kingdom, of which the origin and growth have already been described. Henceforth it was the central figure which occupied the stage of earth, the sole principle of connection among the nations of the world. Like its predecessors, it has been exposed to assaults from without and treachery from within; but as it is unlike them in the nature of its existence, so does it differ from them in the permanence of its sway. Still does it survive, to mock the presumption of those abject and desperate rebels, who think that their petty opposition can defeat the purposes of the Most High. The fall of the fourth monarchy was the hour of its final confirmation. Rome had done it homage, but not till its own ruin was at hand. The new powers which were henceforth to occupy the world found it already in possession. For a change was approaching, more important than the transfer of dynasties, or the alteration of the titles and conditions of sovereign power. The very substance of

[1] A.D. 384.   [2] Gibbon, cap. xxviii. p. 100.

which society consisted—the languages and races of men—were to be renewed. Hitherto the Church had been built of a people, whom the licence and sensuality of Rome, or the pride and false philosophy of Greece, had debased and corrupted. A purer stock was to supply the material for its future extension. A cloud had arisen in the utmost east, which already covered the heavens with its blackness, and indicated the approaching storm. In the interval between Constantine and Theodosius, the Huns, driven from their original seat near the Wall of China, had spread themselves as far as the plains of Muscovy. The Gothic nation, pressed by their superincumbent weight, had already left the German forests, had crossed the Danube, to the number of above a million of persons, and fixed themselves within the dominions of Rome.[1] Other nations, the parents, like them, of the European race, were ready for a final spring upon the empire. Within a few years after the death of Theodosius, the Goths were in possession of Rome.[2] As yet they seemed waiting till the full work was accomplished of that degenerate race, which was to hand on to them the blessings of the Church of God. Its success in the new soil of their rude but manly natures—its conquest over their wild superstition—its dangers from their ignorance, and from that spiritual usurper, the phantom of the departed empire, whose power arose from the associations of its ancient greatness—the final establishment of Christ's kingdom throughout the nations which now make up the central field-plot of the world—its superior purity in those portions of European society which were least mingled with the blood of ancient Rome;—this is the grand subject of modern history.

[1] A.D. 376.   [2] A.D. 410.

CHRONOLOGICAL TABLE.

B.C.
- 4004 Creation.
- 3017 Enoch's translation.
- 2348 Flood.
- 2247 Confusion of tongues. Peleg. The earth divided.
- 2200 Commencement of Nimrod's empire.
- 2008 Peleg's death.
- 2007 Semiramis began to reign.
- 1921 Call of Abraham.
- 1807 Shepherd-kings rule in Egypt.
- 1706 Jacob goes into Egypt.
- 1491 Exodus of Israel.
- 1451 Israelites enter Egypt.
- 1184 Trojan war.
- 1117 Samson's death.
- 1116 Samuel judges Israel.
- 1102 Conquest of Peloponnesus by the Heraclidæ.
- 1048 David king of Israel.
- 1015 Solomon king.
- 975 Jeroboam and Rehoboam kings.
- 918 Ahab king of Israel.
- 884 Lycurgus the Spartan legislator.
- 753 Founding of Rome.
- 747 Death of Sardanapalus. Assyrian empire divided.
- 721 Israel carried captive by Shalmanezer.
- 710 Sennacherib invades Judah.
- 660 Psammetichus introduces Greeks into Egypt.
- 608 Josiah defeated by Pharaoh-Necho.
- 604 Nebuchadnezzar reunites the Assyrian empire. His victory over Necho at Carchemish.
- 587 Jerusalem taken. Captivity.
- 571 Egypt overrun by Nebuchadnezzar.

B.C.
- 569 Pharaoh-Hophra, or Apries, slain by Amasis.
- 560 Pisistratus tyrant of Athens.
- 559 Death of Solon the Athenian legislator.
- 553 Medes and Persians begin to grow in power.
- 548 Crœsus defeated by Cyrus.
- 538 Cyrus takes Babylon.
- 536 Jews return from captivity.
- 522 Usurpation of Smerdis the Magian.
- 521 Darius Hystaspes.
- 519 Darius Hystaspes allows the Temple to be rebuilt.
- 514 Murder of Hipparchus.
- 510 Hippias finally expelled from Athens.
- 509 Kings banished from Rome.
- 504 The Ionian revolt. Sardis burnt.
- 490 Battle of Marathon.
- 485 Xerxes king.
- 481 Xerxes invades Greece.
- 480 Leonidas defends Thermopylæ.
- 479 Battle of Platæa.
- 458 Ahasuerus marries Esther. Ezra sent to Jerusalem.
- 445 Nehemiah sent to Jerusalem.
- 431 Peloponnesian war begins.
- 404 Athens taken by Lysander.
- 401 Expedition of the 10,000 under the younger Cyrus.
- 400 Death of Socrates.
- 390 Rome burnt by the Gauls.
- 371 Battle of Leuctra.
- 362 Battle of Mantinæa.
- 360 Philip king of Macedon.
- 334 Alexander the Great enters Asia. Granicus.
- 333 Battle of Issus.
- 331 Persian empire finally overthrown. Arbela.
- 323 Death of Alexander the Great.
- 301 Battle of Ipsus. Final partition of Alexander's empire.
- 264 First Punic war.
- 248 Second Punic war.
- 216 Battle of Cannæ.
- 197 Philip king of Macedon defeated by the Romans.
- 190 Antiochus defeated by the Romans.
- 170 Antiochus Epiphanes persecutes the Jews.
- 168 Second Macedonian war.
- 149 Third Punic war.
- 146 Romans subdue Greece. Corinth and Carthage destroyed.

Chronological Table.

B.C.
133 Tiberius Gracchus.
121 Caius Gracchus.
101 Marius defeats the Cimbri.
 82 Sylla dictator.
 60 The first triumvirate.
 48 Julius Cæsar makes himself supreme at Rome.   Battle of Pharsalia.
 44 Julius Cæsar assassinated.
 31 Augustus emperor of Rome.   Battle of Actium.
  3 Our Lord's birth.

A.D.
  9 Our Lord goes up to the Temple.
 14 Augustus dies.   Tiberius becomes emperor.
 31 Crucifixion.   St. Paul's conversion.
 32 St. Peter preaches to Cornelius.
 45 St. Paul and St. Barnabas appointed apostles.
 46 Council at Jerusalem.
 54 Nero becomes emperor.
 56 St. Paul carried captive to Rome.
 68 Martyrdom of St. Paul and St. Peter.
 69 Vespasian becomes emperor.
 70 Destruction of Jerusalem.   St. Clement writes to the Corinthians.
 93 St. John at Patmos.   Book of Revelation.
 94 Polycarp appointed bishop of Smyrna by St. John.
 96 St. John writes his Gospel.
 98 Trajan becomes emperor.
100 St. John's death.
107 St. Ignatius martyred.
117 Hadrian becomes emperor.
120 Irenæus is born.
135 Jews banished from Judæa by the Romans.
150 Hegesippus commences his travels.   Tertullian born.
158 St. Polycarp visits Rome in the time of Anicetus.
165 Death of Justin Martyr.
167 St. Polycarp martyred.
168 Montanus the schismatic.
177 Persecutions at Lyons and Vienne.
188 Pantænus goes to India as a missionary.   Pothinus martyred.
199 Tertullian becomes a Montanist.
250 Decian persecution.
258 Cyprian martyred.
284 Diocletian emperor.
286 Maximian appointed emperor.

A.D.
- 298 Marcellus martyred.
- 303 Last persecution begins.
- 305 Diocletian and Maximian abdicate.
- 306 Constantius dies. Constantine becomes Cæsar.
- 312 Constantine marches into Italy, and dethrones Maxentius. Vision of the Cross.
- 313 Edict of Milan, proclaiming toleration to Christians.
- 323 Constantius gives full liberty to Christians.
- 324 Licinius defeated. Constantine sole emperor.
- 325 Council of Nice.
- 337 Constantine dies.
- 361 Julian the apostate.
- 376 The Goths enter Trace.
- 379 Theodosius the Great emperor.
- 381 Second general Council of Constantinople.
- 395 Roman empire divided between Arcadius and Honorius.

INDEX.

ABRAHAM'S call, 16.
Acesius the Novatian, 198.
Alcibiades persuades the Athenians to invade Sicily, 92.
Alexander the Great, 108.
Alexandria founded, 110.
Antiochus Epiphanes, 113.
Apostles, their practice binding on Christians, 143.
———, perpetuity of their office, 151.
Arius, 196.
Ark, long remembered, 6.
Assyrian Empire founded, 13.
Athanasius, 202.
Athenian character, 85.
Athens taken by Sparta, 93.
——— the seat of arts, 95.
——— its low morality shown by the plague, 95.

BABEL, the first attempt at universal empire, 8.
Babylon, its commerce and greatness, 47.
——— taken by Cyrus, 63.
———, Alexander's plans for its restoration, 111.
Bactria, its early wealth, 14.
Balaam, 26.
Bishops, at first the delegates of the apostles, 144.
———, their order fully established by the apostles on the destruction of Jerusalem, 151.

CÆSAR, 129.
Cain, the founder of city-life, 4.
Captivity of Israel, 43.
——— of Judah, 46.
Carthage, 121.
Catholic, impropriety of giving that name to the Romanists, 181.
Chaldeans, their origin, 47.
Church in being before Scripture was written, 169.
Church of England refers to the testimony of the early Fathers, 171.

Index.

Colleges of prophets like cathedrals, the centres of religious worship, 30.
Constantine sought support from the Church, 190.
———, parallel, between his vision and Nebuchadnezzar's, 191.
Constantine refers Church matters to the bishops, 198.
Crœsus consults the oracle at Delphi, 63.
Creed, its antiquity, 170.
———, its last clauses earlier than the Council of Nice, 202.
Cyprian, his statement of the corruption of Christians, 178.
Cyrus's education, 61.
Cyrus the younger invades Persia, 104.

DARIUS HYSTASPES consolidates the Persian State, 67.
Diocletian a refounder of Rome, 184.
——— supposes he has extinguished Christianity, 188.

EGYPT, its early settlement, 19.
——— conquered by Cambyses, 66.
Elijah a restorer of God's service, 41.
Enoch contrasted with Lamech, 4.
Epaminondas, his improvements in the art of war, 106.
Ezra sent to Jerusalem, 103.

GRECIAN character, 76.
Gibbon, his unfairness, 187.

HEGESIPPUS, 166.
Herod's alarm at our Lord's birth, 135.
Homer, 77.
Hosius sent by Constantine to allay Arian disputes, 195.

ISAIAH'S prophecy described, 46.
Israel led out of Egypt, 24.
———, its election typical of the election of Christians at baptism, 24

JEROBOAM causes a schism in the Jewish Church, 40.
Jerusalem, its destruction showed the Jewish polity ended, 150.

KINGDOM of heaven implied an outward system, 141.

LAMECH, meaning of his speech, 4.
Languages show national connection, 8.
Law of Moses, its parts and objects, 25.
———, how it carried on men's minds to the future kingdom, 25.

Index. 213

MACCABEES, 113.
Magian attempt to bring back sceptre to Medes, 67.
Marathon, battle of, 71.
Marcellus's martyrdom, 185.
Martyrdom of St Ignatius, 162.
Montanus, 176.

NEBUCHADNEZZAR, his victories, 50.
———, his dream, 53.
Nice, general council of, 197.
Nicene Creed, how guarded, 200.
Nimrod, the first conqueror, 7.
Nineveh destroyed, 16.
Noah's prophecy, 6.
Novatian, 179.

OPHIR, where, 35.
Oracles of ancients, 62.
Orœtes, a rebellious satrap, 69.

PACIAN, 181.
Palestine, its martyrs, 187.
Peloponnesian war, 89.
Persecution of Diocletian, 186.
Persians superior to the other Orientals, 60.
Persian empire overthrown, 111.
Petra, 35.
Phœnician cities, 32.
Pharaoh-Necho, 21.
Philip of Macedon, 107.
Philosophers, their four chief schools, 100.
Platæa, battle of, 87.
Plato's Polity, 99.
Polycarp's martyrdom, 162.
Prediction of the spiritual kingdom given to the temporal power, 54.
Prophecies, their meaning handed down to the Jewish Church, 113.
Pyramids, 22.
Pythagoras, 97.

ROME built, 120.
Roman empire extended, 124.
Rome the iron empire, 124.
———, its fall, 206.

St CLEMENT'S epistle, 155.
St James, our Lord's cousin, an apostle, but not of the twelve, 144.
St Paul and St Barnabus chosen apostles, 142.
Sacraments, the means of union with Christ's kingdom, 139.
Salamis, battle of, 86.
Samson, celebrated under the name of Hercules, 28.
Samuel, his peculiar commission, 30.
—— founds colleges of prophets, 30.
Sardanapalus, 16.
Schism, its original principle, 175.
Scythians, invaded by Darius, 70.
Semiramis invades India, 14.
Septuagint, 113.
Seth, the father of the spiritual seed, 3.
Sidonians, 32.
Society arose from the family relation, 3.
Socrates, the apostle of conscience, 98.
Solomon, his wisdom and wealth, 31.
Solon, 83.
Sophists, 96.
Spain, its early wealth, 34.
Succession of priesthood, disregarded by Jeroboam, 39.

TEMPLE, our Lord's presence the glory of second, 66.
Ten thousand, their retreat, 105.
Thebes aspires to the rule of Greece, 106.
Themistocles incites the Athenians to defence, 85.
Thermopylæ defended by three hundred Spartans, 82.
Theodosius the Great finally extinguishes paganism in the Roman empire, 203.
—— finally divides the empire, 204.
Tyre, its trade, 34.
——, its sieges, 50, 110.

UNITY of the Church, 132.

XERXES invades Greece, 81.

www.ingramcontent.com/pod-product-compliance
Lightning Source LLC
Chambersburg PA
CBHW051900160426
43198CB00012B/1684